THE FRENCH AND INDIAN WAR

1754–1763

THE FRENCH AND INDIAN WAR

1754–1763

The Imperial Struggle for North America

Seymour I. Schwartz

CASTLE BOOKS

Copyright © 1994 by Simon & Schuster

This edition published by arrangement with and permission of Simon & Schuster by
CASTLE BOOKS
a division of Book, Sales, Inc.
114 Northfield Avenue
Edison, NJ 08837

Printed in China

ISBN 07858-1165-6

Simon & Schuster
Academic Reference Division
15 Columbus Circle
New York, New York 10023

Library of Congress Cataloging-in-Publication Data

Schwartz, Seymour I., 1928–
    The French and Indian War, 1754–1763 : the imperial struggle for
North America / Seymour I. Schwartz.
        p.   cm.
    Includes bibliographical references (p.) and index.
    ISBN 0-13-324237-4 (acid-free paper)
    1. United States—History—French and Indian War, 1755–1763.
I. Title
E199.S376   1994
973.2 ' 6—dc20

Contents

Preface

The French and Indian War, also called the Great War for the Empire, changed the map of North America. The battles that occurred between 1753 and 1760 took more lives than the American War of Independence, making the French and Indian War the bloodiest conflict fought on American soil in the eighteenth century.

The war pitted the French and their Indian allies against the English colonists and their Indian allies along the Atlantic seaboard in an attempt to gain possession of the Ohio Valley. Warriors of legendary and even heroic stature faced each other. The war afforded George Washington his first command of troops. It saw the exploits of Captain Robert Rogers and his Rangers and the dominant role of Sir William Johnson, the great Indian agent in New York colony. It saw the deaths of Louis-Joseph de Montcalm and James Wolfe on the Plains of Abraham as the British captured Quebec. It erased France's political influence from the continent and established English dominance east of the Mississippi and in Canada. And it set the stage for the American Revolution and the establishment of the United States of America.

The French and Indian War: The Imperial Struggle for North America presents, for the first time, a description of the battles and engagements of the war complemented by contemporary maps, drawings, and engravings of troop movements, views of forts, and portraits of participants. This book contains 118 illustrations, many from my own collection, as well as from public and private sources in the United States, Canada, and Europe.

There is an analogy between the way in which this book came about and how paper was made in the eighteenth century. The paper was made of rag. The rags were shredded and pulverized in water and the resulting emulsion poured into a frame that was crossed vertically and horizontally by closely placed strands of wire to which the emulsion would attach. Lift up a piece of paper bearing the impression of an antique map and the positions of these so-called lay lines are apparent. In like manner, several strands cross in the making of this book. They cannot be viewed directly, but they exist nevertheless.

The first strand is the need for a hobby for an academic surgeon dedicated to his vocation. The great physician Sir William Osler said, "No man is really happy or safe without [a hobby]." Thirty years ago the history of cartography became my hobby. Then I became a collector of maps. The first items I acquired were relatively inconsequential sixteenth- and seventeenth-century maps, generally focusing on North America. Then I developed a theme for my collection: I would acquire maps that were critical in the evolution of knowledge about the North American continent printed or drawn before 1800. It is this focus that converted a series of acquisitions into a meaningful collection.

The next strand was the infusion of scholarship. Scholarship provides the blood flow that vitalizes the inert graphic representation of geography. In 1624 John Smith wrote, "Geography without History seemeth as a carkasse without motion." Further, writing is not merely a distillate of scholarship; when it is intended for publication, permanence of print mandates exactness. I found this to be true with my book, *The Mapping of North America*, the product of eight years of scholarly effort and writing.

The final strand was simply to look at my collection and note that I had a significant number of maps relating to the French and Indian War. No work had provided an in-depth consideration of the cartography of that conflict. In fact, most people plead ignorance of that war; only a few can place James Fenimore Cooper's *Last of the Mohicans, Deerslayer,* and *Pathfinder* in their correct historical context. *The French and Indian War: The Imperial Struggle for North America* addresses that void.

I appreciate the editorial assistance provided by Amy Wilkin in assembling the material in this book. I want to thank Royal Chamberlain and Martha Smith for their help in photographing the maps. Thanks are also due to Charles E. Smith, president of Simon & Schuster's Academic Reference Division; Stephen Wagley, senior editor at Simon & Schuster; and Kerri Lewis, the designer of this book, at A Good Thing.

Seymour I. Schwartz

THE FRENCH
AND INDIAN WAR

1754–1763

Introduction

*I*n the eighteenth century, the North American continent was the seat of two major conflicts that resulted in the birth of the United States of America. The War of Independence, also known as the War of the Revolution, extended from 1775 through 1781 and was the definitive event. But the French and Indian War, which took place between 1754 and 1763, set the stage for the Revolution.

The term French and Indian War is the most popular title in America for a conflict called the Seven Years' War in Europe, where it lasted from 1756 to 1763; it has also been designated the Great War for the Empire by the historian Lawrence Henry Gipson. What began as a struggle over territorial rights between British colonists and French settlers became part of an international war between the great powers, the first of the modern world wars, with campaigns in Europe, India, Africa, the West Indies, and the North American continent. The longest and bloodiest war in North America in the eighteenth century resulted in British domination of the continent, albeit domination that was per-

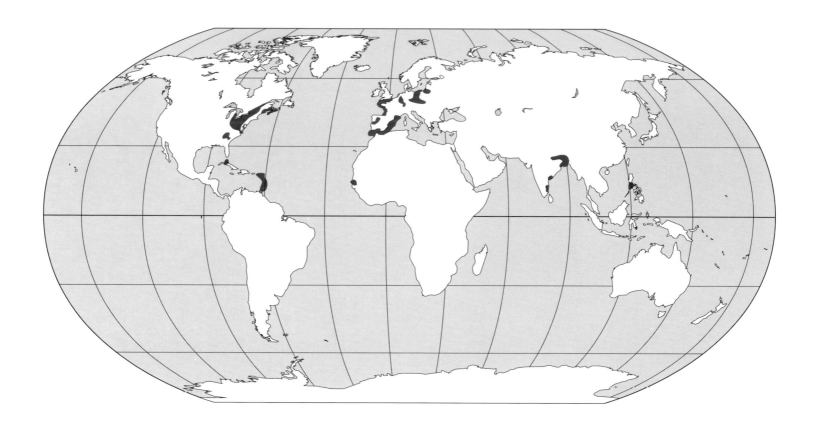

meated with dissatisfaction and dissent on the part of the colonists. France lost its dominions on two continents and Great Britain became the world's premier sea power and colonial power.

British claims to the continent were based on the fact that it had been discovered in 1498 by John Cabot (Giovanni Gaboto) sailing under the flag of England. In the first half of the seventeenth century grants were made by King James I to the London Company and the Bristol Company of all land from 34 to 45 degrees north latitude (approximately from Cape Fear, North Carolina, to Liscomb, Nova Scotia) from the Atlantic Ocean, including all coastal islands, to the west "indefinitely." Subsequent grants were made by royal charter to the Virginia Company and Grand Council of Massachusetts for lands extending from "sea to sea." In the latter half of the seventeenth century, the Crown established the province of Carolina as a sea-to-sea grant and granted William Penn a charter.

France, however, regarded itself as possessor of all disputed western lands in North America, including the Ohio Valley, based on the discoveries of René-Robert Cavelier de La Salle in 1682 and prior explorations by Jacques Marquette, Louis Jolliet (or Joliet) and others. The French had a lengthy history of establishing forts along the Mississippi River, the Great Lakes, and at strategic sites to protect their commercial interests. In 1672, they built a fort on the north side of the east entrance of Lake Ontario, and in 1673, another fort at Michilimackinac, where Lakes Superior, Huron, and Michigan come together. A fort was erected at Niagara in 1684 on the strait between Lakes Erie and Ontario. In 1732, they built a modern fort at Louisbourg on Cape Breton to control the entrance to the Saint Lawrence River. Even after the Treaty of Aix-la-Chapelle in 1748 confirmed the Treaty of Utrecht of 1713 establishing the boundaries of the Hudson's Bay Company, the French continued to establish forts such as Fort Beaubassin in Acadia and Crown Point on Lake Champlain. Forts were also erected on the Ouabache (Wabash), Ohio, Mississippi, and Missouri Rivers.

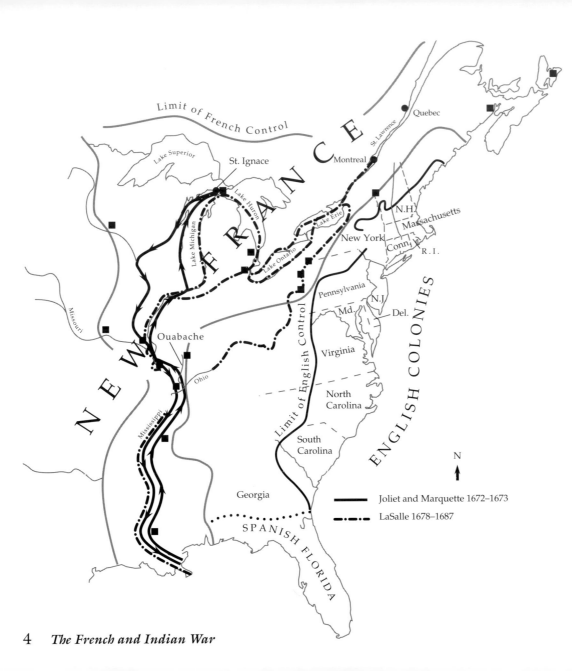

Routes of
French Explorers.

Limit of French Control

Lake Superior

St. Ignace

Lake Huron

Lake Michigan

N E W

F R A N C E

Quebec

St. Lawrence

Montreal

Lake Erie

Lake Ontario

New York

N.H.

Massachusetts

Conn.

R.I.

Missouri

Ouabache

Ohio

Mississippi

Limit of English Control

Pennsylvania

N.J.

Md.

Del.

Virginia

North
Carolina

South
Carolina

Georgia

E N G L I S H   C O L O N I E S

N

Joliet and Marquette 1672–1673

LaSalle 1678–1687

S P A N I S H   F L O R I D A

Figure 1.

Marquis Duquesne.
Ange, Sieur de Menneville, the Marquis Duquesne, Chevalier of the Royal and Military Order of St. Louis, Captain of His Majesty's Ships, Governor and Lieutenant General for the King in All New France (1752–1755). (Courtesy of the Public Archives of Canada.)

Figure 2.

Robert Dinwiddie.
Lieutenant Governor of Virginia (1751–1758). (Courtesy of the National Portrait Gallery, London.)

The British moved to protect their own interests by building forts and bases to counter French activities. In 1727, following the purchase of land from the Indians, Fort Oswego was constructed on the shores of Lake Ontario. In 1749, Halifax was established in Acadia to rival Louisbourg. Of even greater consequence was the expansion of British claims by land purchases and the granting of territory within the Ohio Valley to the Ohio Company, with the condition that a settlement be developed to give evidence of a permanent presence.

In 1749, Captain Pierre-Joseph Céleron de Blainville set out from Montreal and proceeded to the shores of the Allegheny and Ohio Rivers demanding that the British traders lower the flags from their trading post and retreat to the eastern slopes of the Appalachians. A year later, as the conflict of interests became more apparent, a commission representing both sides met in Paris. No progress was made, and the meeting was rapidly adjourned. In June 1752 Charles Leglande, a French Indian agent, led an Indian raid that destroyed a British trading center at Pickawillany on the Upper Greater Miami River in present-day Ohio. On July 1, 1752, the Marquis Duquesne (Figure 1) landed at Quebec to become the governor-general of New France, with specific instructions to take possession of the territories of the Ohio Valley. In 1753, French forts were built at Presque Isle (Erie, Pa.) and on the Rivière aux Boeufs (Waterford, Pa.). On the British side, Lieutenant Governor Robert Dinwiddie of Virginia (Figure 2) granted 1.5 million acres of land in the Ohio Valley to several prominent Virginia families. The stage was set and the scenery put in place for the curtain to be raised on the French and Indian War.

2

1753

George Washington's Mission

Chronology

October 31	George Washington sets out from Williamsburg, Va.
November 25	Washington reaches the Monongahela River.
December 11–12	Washington at Fort Le Boeuf.
January 16, 1754	Washington returns to Williamsburg

The war in 1753.

The assignment of a given date or even a year as the beginning of a war that was initiated without formal declaration but rather as a series of scattered conflicts is arbitrary. Reason and romance dictate that a cartographic history of the French and Indian War begin in the latter half of 1753, because that period brings into focus both a major American hero and a memorable map.

When Lieutenant Governor Robert Dinwiddie of Virginia learned that the French had built two forts on the Rivière aux Boeufs near the south shore of Lake Erie, in what is presently Waterford, Pennsylvania, and had fifteen hundred regular troops stationed in those parts he hastened to assert the rights of Virginia and England. To accomplish this he dispatched a twenty-one-year old major in the Virginia militia, George Washington (Figure 3), on a journey of more than five hundred miles to the garrison at Fort Le Boeuf to insist upon a peaceful departure of the French.

According to his journal (Figure 4), Washington set out on his mission from Williamsburg on Wednesday, October 31, 1753. The following day he arrived at Fredericksburg, where he engaged his fencing instructor, Jacob Van Braam, to serve as his interpreter. After taking on provisions at Alexandria and Winchester, he proceeded to the Ohio Company's storehouse at Wills Creek, where he hired a seasoned frontiersman, Christopher Gist, as his guide, along with four other traders to accompany him. On November 25th, the group reached Frazier's trading post at the mouth of Turtle Creek on the Monongahela River. Here they received word of the death of the Sieur de Marin, who had been in charge of Fort Le Boeuf, and heard that the major part of the French troops had moved to winter quarters. At that time Washington surveyed the fork of the Ohio River at the Allegheny and Monongahela Rivers. He suggested in his journal and on his map (Figure 5) a location for a proposed fort that he deemed preferable to one put forth previously for the Ohio Company by George Mercer (Figure 6). It was at Washington's suggestion that the building of Fort George, which would become Fort Duquesne and eventually Fort Pitt, was initiated at this site.

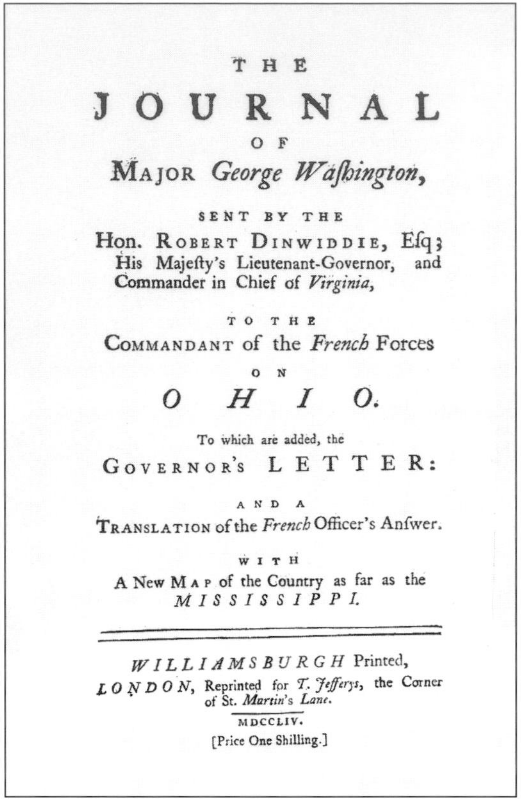

THE
JOURNAL
OF
Major *George Washington,*

SENT BY THE

Hon. ROBERT DINWIDDIE, Eſq;
His Majeſty's Lieutenant-Governor, and
Commander in Chief of *Virginia,*

TO THE

COMMANDANT of the *French* Forces

ON

O H I O.

To which are added, the

GOVERNOR'S LETTER:

AND A

TRANSLATION of the *French* Officer's Anſwer.

WITH

A New MAP of the Country as far as the
MISSISSIPPI.

WILLIAMSBURGH Printed,
LONDON, Reprinted for *T. Jefferys,* the Corner
of St. *Martin's* Lane.
MDCCLIV.
[Price One Shilling.]

Figure 3.

George Washington.
By Charles Willson Peale
(1772). The earliest portrait
of Washington painted
from life shows him in the
uniform of a colonel in
the Virginia Regiment.
(Courtesy Washington
and Lee University,
Lexington, Va.)

Figure 4.

Washington's journal.
This record was published
initially in Williamsburg in
January 1754 and shortly
thereafter in London
by Thomas Jefferys.
(Private Collection.)

Figure 5.

Washington's sketch map. This map, discovered in London in 1981, shows the country Washington traversed from October 31, 1753, through January 16, 1754. 46 x 36cm. (Private Collection.)

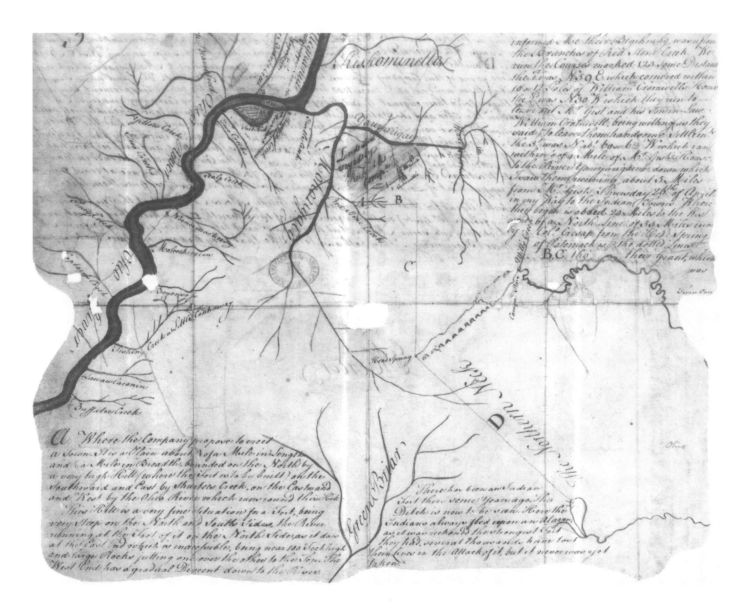

Figure 6.

Mercer's map.
Map of Ohio Company's lands on Ohio River with proposed location of fort and settlement. Signed "G. Mercer." In notes on the map and on the back Mercer states:

> It is a Plain about 3/4 of a Mile in Length and 1/2 Mile in Breadth, bounded on the North by a very high Hill (where the Fort is to be built) on the Southward and East by Shurtees [Chartier's] Creek, on Eastward and West by the Ohio River which runs around this Hill.

This Hill is a very fine Situation for a Fort, being very Steep on the North and South sides, the River running at the Foot of it on the North side as it does on the East End which is inaccessible, being near 100 Feet High and large Rocks jutting one over the other to the Top. The West end has a gradual Descent down to the River.

C. 1753. 37 x 46cm. (Courtesy Public Record Office, London.) Schematic representation is at right.

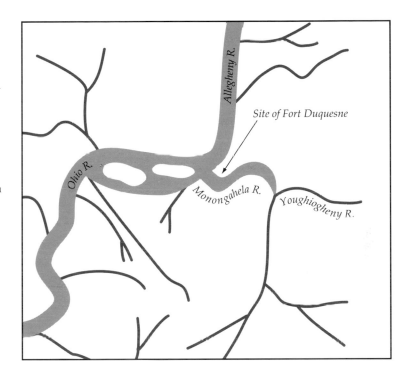

Washington continued on to Loggs Town or Logstown (now Cambridge Springs, Pa.) to meet the Seneca chief Monakaduto, known to the colonists as Half King. It was there on November 25th that Washington saw French uniforms (Figure 7) for the first time when four deserters entered the camp. On December 11th, Washington and his fellow travelers, including Half King, arrived at Fort Le Boeuf. The following day, Washington presented Lieutenant Governor Dinwiddie's letter (Figure 8) to the recently appointed French commander, the Legardeur de St. Pierre de Repentigny, who had arrived at the fort only a week before. On December 15th, St. Pierre indicated that he was unable to comply with the request to abandon the garrison and that the governor's letter would be transmitted to the Marquis Duquesne (Figure 9).

Washington and his party left the fort on December 16th. Ten days later, just after passing a "place called Murdering Town," Washington or Gist was fired at by one of a party of Indians who had laid in wait for them. Washington proceeded rapidly and on January 16, 1754, he arrived at Williamsburg. The following day he transmitted his report to the council. The journal chronicling the experiences of Major George Washington was

Figure 7.

French uniform.
A soldier of the Regiment of the French province of Béarn. C. 1756. (Courtesy Public Archives of Canada.)

Figure 8.

Dinwiddie's letter.
A "copy of his Honour the Governor's Letter, to the Commandant of the French Forces on the Ohio, sent by Major Washington," as it appeared in Washington's journal. (Private Collection.)

COPY *of his Honour the* GOVERNQR's *Letter, to the Commandant of the* French *Forces on the* OHIO, *fent by Major* Wafhington.

SIR,

THE Lands upon the River *Ohio*, in the Weftern Parts of the Colony of *Virginia*, are fo notorioufly known to be the Property of the Crown of *Great-Britain* ; that it is a Matter of equal Concern and Surprize to me, to hear that a Body of *French* Forces are erecting Fortreffes, and making Settlements upon that River, within his Majefty's Dominions.

The many and repeated Complaints I have received of thefe Acts of Hoftility, lay me under the Neceffity, of fending, in the Name of the King my Mafter, the Bearer hereof, *George Wafhington,* Efq; one of the Adjutants General of the Forces of this Dominion; to complain to you of the Encroachments thus made, and of the Injuries done to the Subjects of *Great-Britain*, in open Violation of the Law of Nations, and the Treaties now fubfifting between the two Crowns.

If thefe Facts are true, and you fhall think fit to juftify your Proceedings, I muft defire you to acquaint me, by whofe Authority and Inftructions you have lately marched from *Canada*, with an armed Force ; and invaded the King of *Great-Britain*'s

Britain's Territories, in the Manner complained of? that according to the Purport and Refolution of your Anfwer, I may act agreeably to the Commiffion I am honoured with, from the King my Mafter.

However Sir, in Obedience to my Inftructions, it becomes my Duty to require your peaceable Departure ; and that you would forbear profecuting a Purpofe fo interruptive of the Harmony and good Underftanding, which his Majefty is defirous to continue and cultivate with the moft Chriftian King.

I perfuade myfelf you will receive and entertain Major *Wafhington* with the Candour and Politenefs natural to your Nation ; and it will give me the greateft Satisfaction, if you return him with an Anfwer fuitable to my Wifhes for a very long and lafting Peace between us. I have the Honour to fubfcribe myfelf,

SIR,

Your moft obedient,

Humble Servant,

ROBERT DINWIDDIE.

Williamfburgh, in *Virginia,*
Octo*ber* 31ft, 1753.

TRANS-

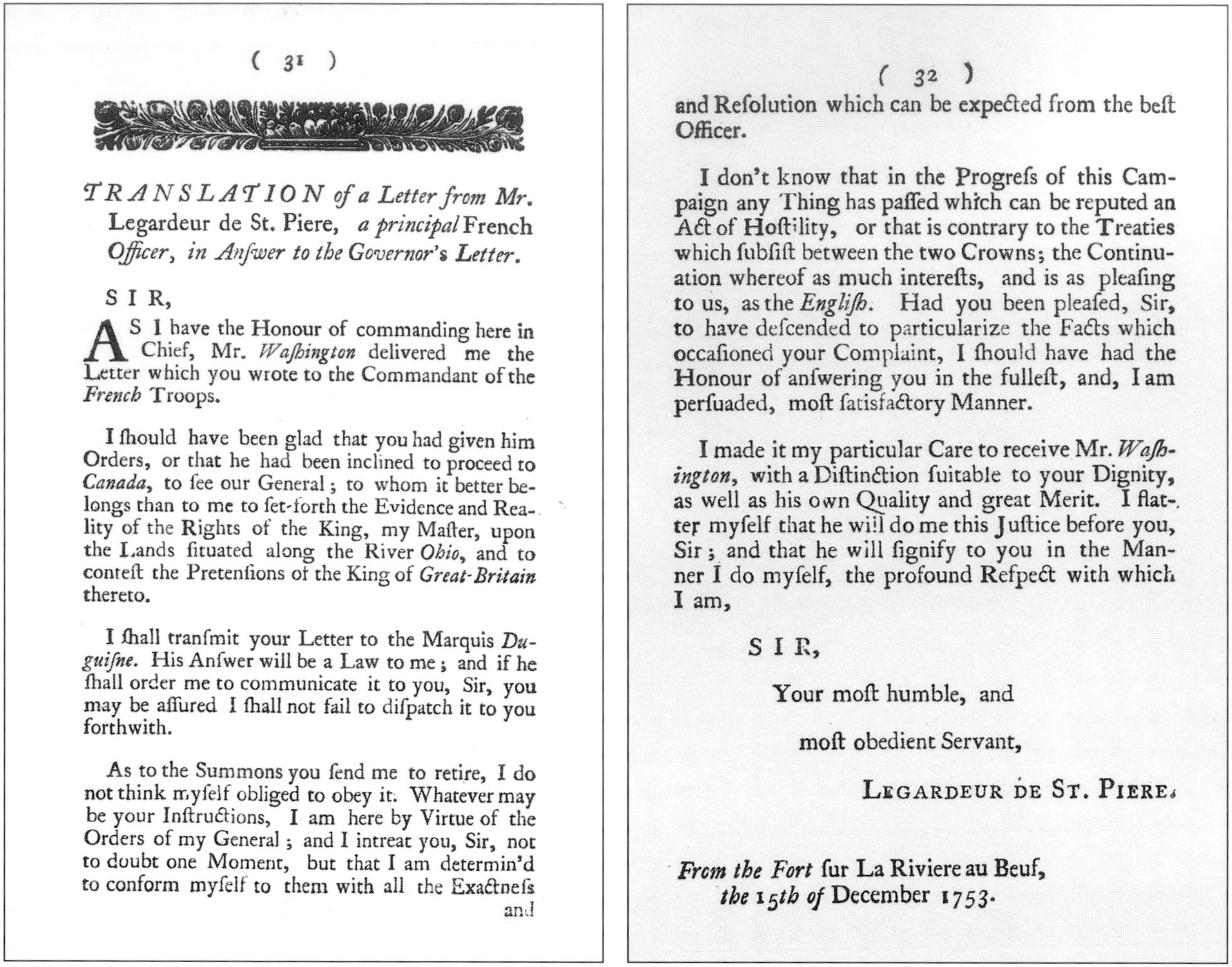

*TRANSLATION of a Letter from Mr.
Legardeur de St. Piere, a principal French
Officer, in Answer to the Governor's Letter.*

S I R,

AS I have the Honour of commanding here in
Chief, Mr. *Washington* delivered me the
Letter which you wrote to the Commandant of the
French Troops.

I should have been glad that you had given him
Orders, or that he had been inclined to proceed to
Canada, to see our General; to whom it better be-
longs than to me to set-forth the Evidence and Rea-
lity of the Rights of the King, my Master, upon
the Lands situated along the River *Ohio*, and to
contest the Pretensions of the King of *Great-Britain*
thereto.

I shall transmit your Letter to the Marquis *Du-
guisne*. His Answer will be a Law to me; and if he
shall order me to communicate it to you, Sir, you
may be assured I shall not fail to dispatch it to you
forthwith.

As to the Summons you send me to retire, I do
not think myself obliged to obey it. Whatever may
be your Instructions, I am here by Virtue of the
Orders of my General; and I intreat you, Sir, not
to doubt one Moment, but that I am determin'd
to conform myself to them with all the Exactness
and

and Resolution which can be expected from the best
Officer.

I don't know that in the Progress of this Campaign any Thing has passed which can be reputed an
Act of Hostility, or that is contrary to the Treaties
which subsist between the two Crowns; the Continu-
ation whereof as much interests, and is as pleasing
to us, as the *English*. Had you been pleased, Sir,
to have descended to particularize the Facts which
occasioned your Complaint, I should have had the
Honour of answering you in the fullest, and, I am
persuaded, most satisfactory Manner.

I made it my particular Care to receive Mr. *Washington*, with a Distinction suitable to your Dignity,
as well as his own Quality and great Merit. I flat-
ter myself that he will do me this Justice before you,
Sir; and that he will signify to you in the Manner I do myself, the profound Respect with which
I am,

S I R,

Your most humble, and

most obedient Servant,

LEGARDEUR DE ST. PIERE.

From the Fort sur La Riviere au Beuf,
the 15th of December 1753.

Figure 9.

St. Pierre's reply.
A "Translation of a Letter
from Mr. Legardeur de
St. Piere, a principal French
Officer, in Answer to the
Governor's Letter," as it
appeared in Washington's
journal. (Private Collection.)

initially published in Williamsburg, then sent to England with copies of a manuscript map depicting the geography.

The most widely reproduced of these manuscript maps (Figure 10) resides in the Public Record Office in London. On it a descriptive note enclosed in a rectangle (Figure 11) states:

> The French are now coming from the Forts on Lake Erie & on the Creek to Venango to erect another Fort—And from these they design to the Forks of the Monongahele and to the Logs Town, and so to continue down the River building at the most convenient places in order to prevent our settlements yea. NB. A Little below Shanapins Town in the Fork is the place where we are going immediately to build a Fort as it commands the Ohio and Monongahele—

Another almost identical copy has now come to light (see Figure 5). It is more primitive in that it includes only five arrows showing the directions of streams, in contrast to the ten arrows on the Public Record Office copy and the two houses at "Mr. Gist's new Sett." rather than the three on the PRO copy. Shortly after its arrival in London, Washington's journal was reprinted by the British publisher Thomas Jefferys, including a "Map of the Western parts of the Colony of VIRGINIA as far as the Mississipi[sic]" (Figure 12).

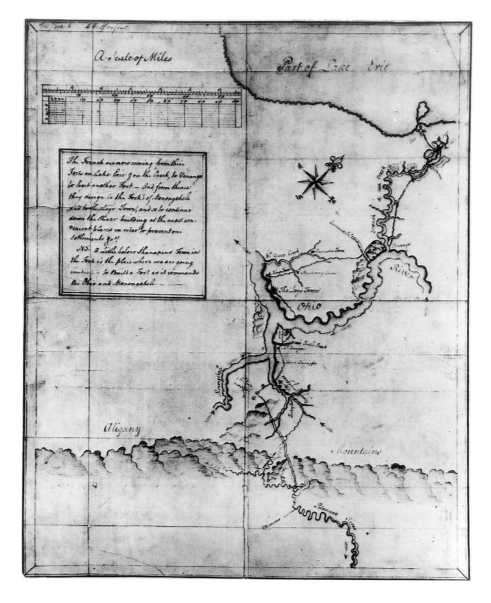

Figure 10.
Washington's campaign.
This sketch map by George
Washington shows the
country traversed in
1753–1754. 46 x 36cm.
(Courtesy Public Record
Office, London.)

Figure 11.

Detail of Figure 10.
An enlargement of the text on map shown in Figure 10. (Courtesy Public Record Office, London.)

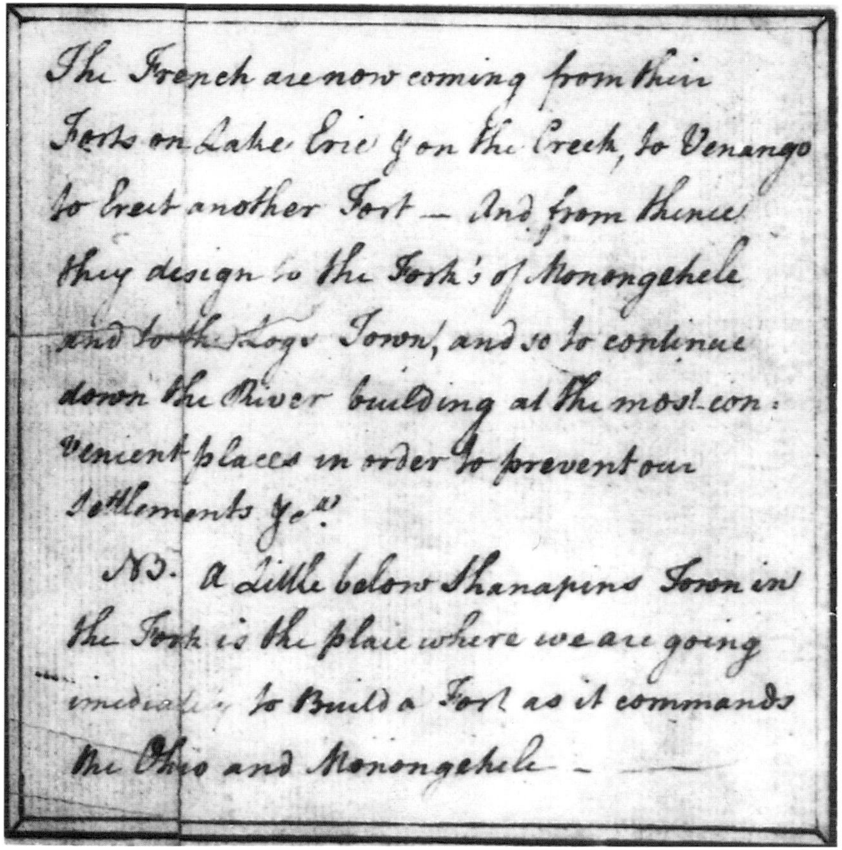

The French are now coming from their Forts on Lake Erie & on the Creek, to Venango to Erect another Fort — And from thence they design to the Fork's of Monongehele and to the Logs Town, and so to continue down the River building at the most con: venient places in order to prevent our Settlements &c.

N3. A Little below Shanapins Town in the Fork is the place where we are going imediately to Build a Fort as it commands the Ohio and Monongehele —

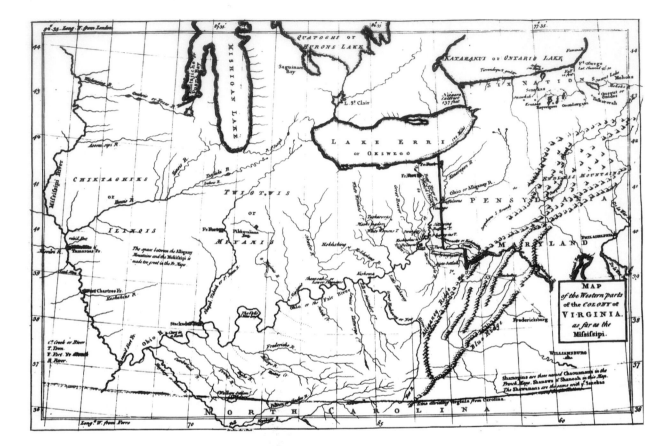

Figure 12.

Jefferys' map.
Map of the Western parts of the Colony of VIRGINIA as far as the Mississipi. This map appeared in the London edition of George Washington's journal. Thomas Jefferys, 1754. 23 x 36cm. (Private Collection.)

3

1754
The First Engagements

Chronology

February 14	Virginia's House of Burgesses appropriates £10,000 for western expedition against the French.
May 28	French and Indian War formally begins with George Washington's force defeating the French contingent, then establishing Fort Necessity.
June 14	English-Iroquois trade conference in Albany, N.Y., works to prevent breakup of alliance.

July 3	French take Fort Necessity.
July 17	Washington returns to Williamsburg, is faulted by House of Burgesses for failed campaign, and resigns commission. Parliament votes additional forces after word received in England of Fort Necessity defeat.

*F*ollowing Washington's report to the governing council, the province of Virginia moved rapidly to limit encroachments by the French. Lieutenant Governor Robert Dinwiddie convened the House of Burgesses on February 14th, at which time an appropriation of £10,000 was voted to raise and equip the necessary troops. Washington was promoted to Lieutenant Colonel and placed second in command to Colonel Joshua Fry, an elderly officer in the Virginia militia who had with Thomas Jefferson's father Peter made in 1751 a highly regarded map of Virginia and Maryland (Figure 13).

Virginians versus French in the West

The fur trader William Trent was commissioned as captain and charged with recruiting a force of men to build a fort at the forks of the Ohio River on the site that Washington had previously designated optimal for achieving control of the region. On February 17th they began to build a redoubt to be named Fort Prince George, in honor of the heir to the British throne. On April 18th, when the building had reached a height just above ground level, Captain Pierre de Contrecoeur, the commandant of French forts on the Ohio, appeared with over five hundred well-armed troops and forced the Virginians to surrender the site. The French proceeded to complete the structure and named it Fort Duquesne.

IROQUOIS

Fort Halifax
Winslow

Fort Western
Augusta

Albany ●

Sandusky ▪

Fort Duquesne
Pittsburgh ▪

Fort Necessity
▪ *Farmington*

Fort Cumberland
Cumberland

Alexandria ●

The war in 1754.

Meanwhile, on April 2nd, Washington led his troops westward out of Alexandria, Virginia, and arrived at Wills Creek two weeks later. Shortly after his arrival, he received word of the surrender of Fort Prince George. Washington established an encampment at Great Meadows, about fifty miles northwest of Wills Creek and sixty-five miles southwest of the forks of the Ohio. On May 25th, Colonel Fry led two companies out of Winchester, Virginia, toward Wills Creek. During that march he fell from his horse and died, leaving Washington in command.

While Fry had been proceeding westward, Washington received word at Great Meadows that a contingent of French troops was in the vicinity planning an attack. At seven in the morning of May 28th, while the French were preparing breakfast, Washington and his men attacked the French encampment. After an engagement of only some fifteen minutes, the French surrendered. Among the dead was the young French commander, Ensign Joseph Coulon de Villiers, the Sieur de Jumonville, the victim of a blow from Half King's tomahawk. Twenty-one prisoners were taken, but one man escaped to Fort Duquesne, where he reported the event. Washington led his men back to the encampment at Great Meadows. The French later maintained that the bullets discharged by the English on this occasion informally initiated the French and Indian War.

Anticipating an immediate reprisal by the French, Washington had his force of 180 men build a stockade at their campsite of Great Meadows. This structure, named Fort Necessity, was in the shape of a circle about 53 feet in diameter designed to accommodate approximately fifty men, and contained a small storehouse (Figure 14). (In 1771, Washington would purchase 234 acres of the Great Meadows, for slightly over £35.) On June 3rd, Washington received news of Fry's death.

Led by Captain Louis Coulon Ecuyer, Sieur de Villiers, the half-brother of the slain Sieur de Jumonville, seven hundred French soldiers and more than 350 Indians left Fort Duquesne and on the morning of July 3rd attacked Fort Necessity. (The area is shown in a contemporary map in Figure 15.) The battle lasted about four hours. That evening the

Figure 13.

Fry and Jefferson map. "A Map of the Most Inhabited part of Virginia, containing the whole province of Maryland with Part of Pensilvania, New Jersey and North Carolina." Joshua Fry and Peter Jefferson (1751). Engraving, 77 x 123cm. (Courtesy Tracy W. Gregor Library, University of Virginia.)

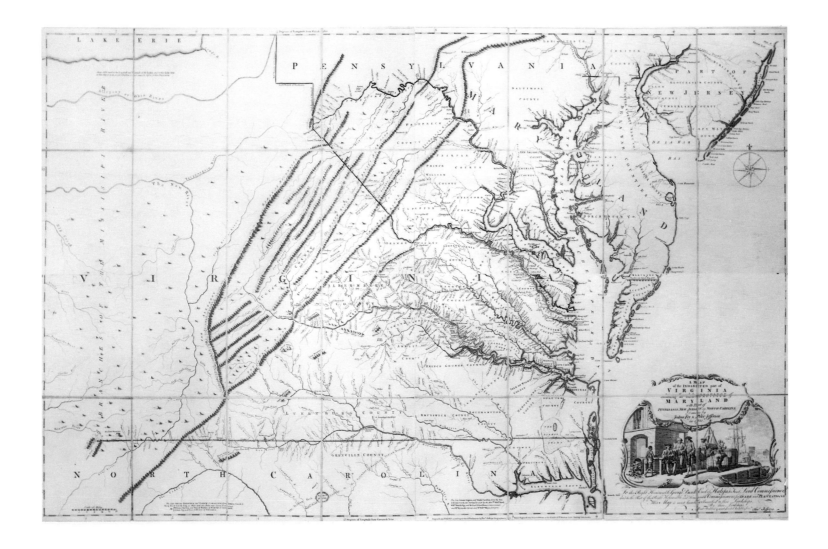

Figure 14.

Fort Necessity.
Re-created Fort Necessity, on the Great Meadows, southwest of Fort Duquesne. (Courtesy National Park Service.)

French commander offered terms of surrender under which the English would be permitted to return home, because the two countries were not at war. Washington, realizing that his force was significantly outmanned, accepted the terms, and on July 4th the French flag was raised. The English buried their thirty-one men who had died. Captains Robert Stobo, who would in 1759 serve in the Quebec campaign, and Jacob Van Braam were taken hostage, to be held until the previously captured French troops were returned.

The articles of capitulation became the focus of considerable attention. Translated from the French by Van Braam for Washington's signature, they contained the word *l'assassinat* (murder), which the French contended represented a confession that Jumonville had

Figure 15.

A contemporary map of the Fort Necessity area. "Captain Snow's Scetch of the Country by Himself, and the best accounts He could receive from the Indian Traders 1754." Manuscript, 21 x 34cm. The map identifies the "Meadows where the Battle was fought." Fort Necessity is marked "E. Ft." At the junction of the Monongahela and Allegheny Rivers is a fort where it is noted that "120 Sqr. Trent drove out by ye French, 1754." (Courtesy Library of Congress.)

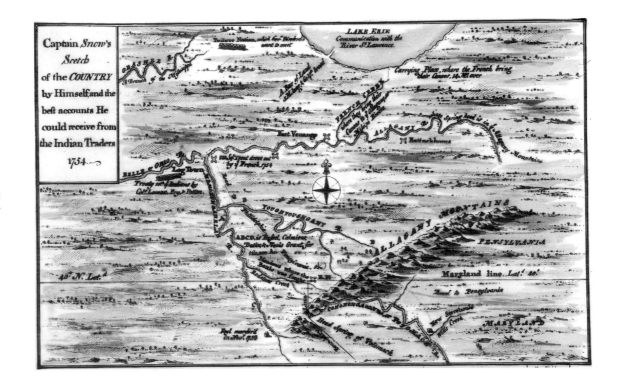

been murdered. The English, however, insisted that the phrase be translated as "the defeat" of Jumonville.

During their return to Fort Duquesne, the French burned Gist's settlement and the Ohio Company's storehouse at Wills Creek. At this point no English flag was flying west of the Allegheny Mountains.

Stobo arrived at Fort Duquesne on July 8th. About a month later he smuggled out two letters, using a Mohawk Indian named Moses the Song, who carried them to George

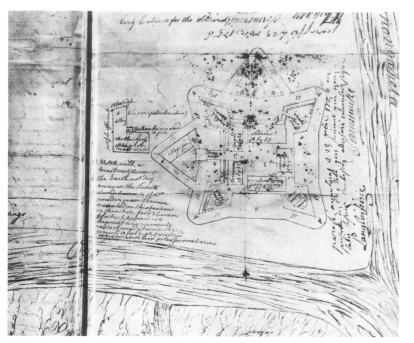

Croghan, a trader, who in turn sent them on to the commander at Wills Creek. One of these contained a map detailing the plan of Fort Duquesne (Figure 16). The first printed plan of the fort appeared in 1755 (Figure 17).

Van Braam was taken to Canada with Stobo and also sent to prison in Quebec. He escaped and was recaptured. He was moved to Montreal, where he was placed under house confinement. Van Braam was freed by the British troops when Montreal capitulated, returned to Williamsburg, and entered the regular British Army.

During his retreat from Fort Necessity, Washington stopped at Wills Creek, where he assisted in building a fort that was later named Fort Cumberland. The fort appears on a contemporary map of the region (Figure 18). On July 17th, he arrived back in Williamsburg and gave an account of the engagement on the Great Meadows. The Virginia council ascribed much of the failure of the mission to faulty leadership on Washington's part. He therefore tendered his resignation, which was accepted, and left Williamsburg November 2nd.

Figure 16.

Fort Duquesne.
The scale map of Fort Duquesne was smuggled out of the fort by Robert Stobo by means of a Mohawk named Moses the Song. Some of the annotations relate to representations by the French at Stobo's trial later in Montreal. Manuscript. (Courtesy Montreal Archives.)

Figure 17.

First printed map of Fort Duquesne. "Plan of Fort Le Quesne. Built by the French, at the Fork of the Ohio and Monongahela in 1754." [Robert Stobo], Robert Sayer, and Thomas Jefferys, London. Engraved, 33 x 30 cm. (Courtesy William Clements Library, University of Michigan.)

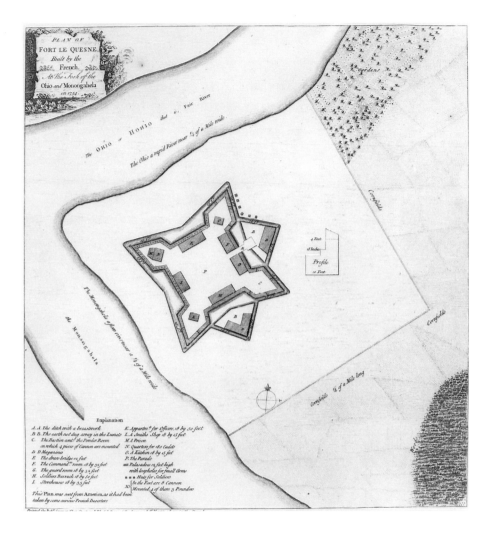

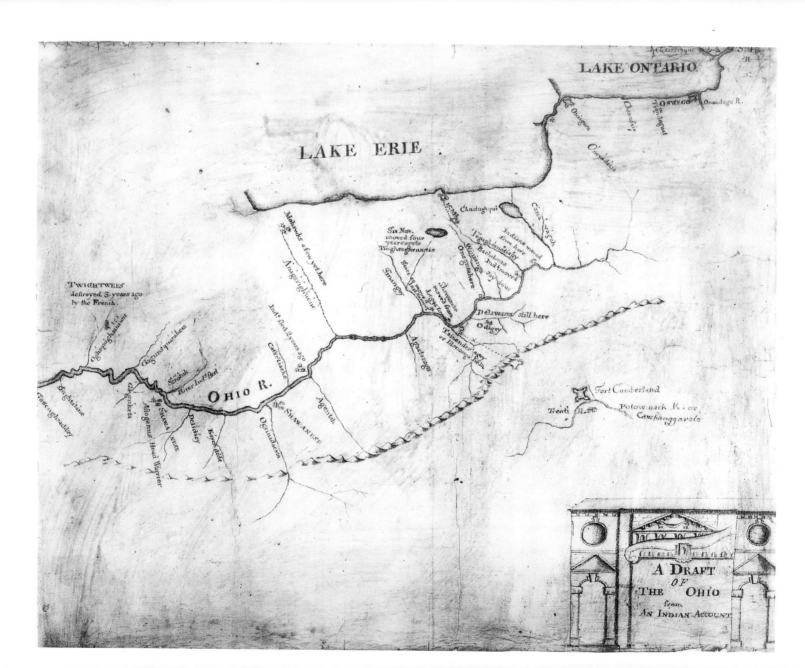

LAKE ONTARIO

LAKE ERIE

OSWEGO · Onandaga R.

Chadaghqui

Six Nats.
moved four
years ago to
Twightwighwunnie

Indians moved
from here

Delawares still here

TWIGHTWEES
destroyed 3. years ago
by the French.

OHIO R.

The SHAWANESE

Fort Cumberland

Trent's Potowmack R. or
Cawhanggarelo

A DRAFT
OF
THE OHIO
from
AN INDIAN ACCOUNT

Figure 18.

The Ohio Valley.
"A Draft of The Ohio
from An Indian Account."
[Anonymous, c. 1755]
Manuscript, 34 x 42 cm.
This map was found in
the collection of General
Thomas Gage. (Courtesy
William Clements Library,
University of Michigan.)
Schematic representation
is at right.

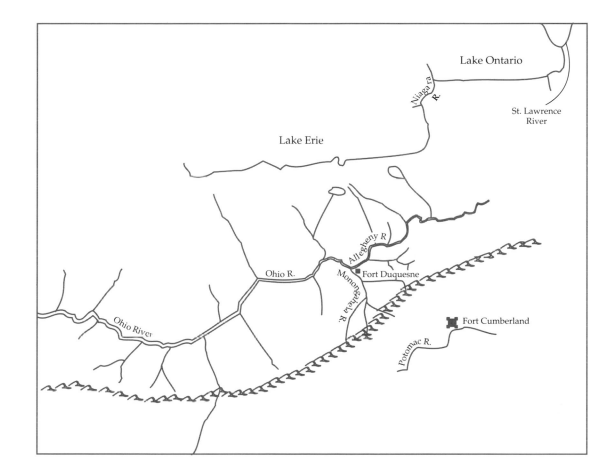

The Northern Theater

In the northern colonies of New York and Massachusetts, the great Mohawk sachem Tiyanoga, known to the English as Hendrick, who had gone as part of a legation to London in 1710 (Figure 19), threatened that the Five Nations of the Iroquois would terminate their alliance with the English unless the existing trade agreements were improved. The board of trade ordered all the colonies involved in English-Iroquois relations to meet as a group with the Five Nations and work out an acceptable policy. Lieutenant Governor James De Lancey of New York convened the meeting in Albany on June 14th. At this meeting Benjamin Franklin proposed a plan for a federation of all the colonies in British America under a single legislature and a President General appointed by the king. It was also at this meeting that William Johnson (Figure 20) was reinstated as Indian agent for New York, because he had the greatest influence with the Iroquois, who gave him the name Warraghiyagey. Although the Albany conference failed to accomplish any of its goals, it did elevate the stature of Johnson, who would play a major role in the ensuing war.

Figure 19.

Tiyanoga. Hendrick, as he was known to the English, as etched from an original drawing by Thomas Jefferys in 1756. (Courtesy New-York Historical Society.)

Figure 20.

Superintendant of Indian Affairs. Sir William Johnson (1715–1774) by John Wollaston, ca. 1750. (Courtesy Albany Institute of History and Art.)

In Massachusetts, Lieutenant Governor William Shirley had Fort Western built in 1754, seventy-three miles from the mouth of the Kennebec River, and Fort Halifax, fifty-four miles downriver, to protect against Indian attacks (Figure 21). The same year, the French built a fort at Sandusky, on the south shore of Lake Erie, to control portage routes and replace the small log structure there known as Fort Niagara. Its engineer, the Chevalier Chausse-gros de Léry referred to it as the "best and strongest bastion of all this wilderness empire of New France."

When news of the capitulation of Fort Necessity reached London and it was also learned that French troops had embarked for Canada with orders to attack Fort Oswego, Parliament voted monies to expand the army and navy and send more troops to Virginia and the northern colonies.

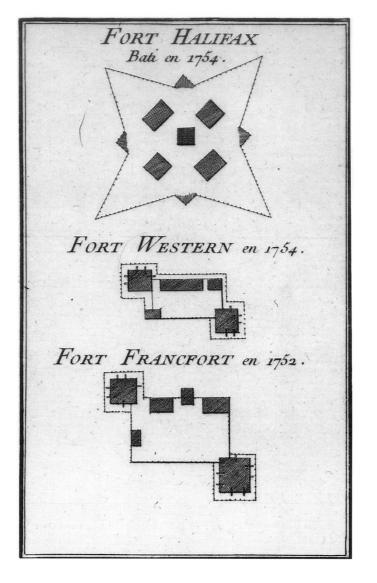

Figure 21.

Three forts.
"Fort Halifax, Bati en 1754. Fort Western en 1754. Fort Francfort en 1752." Engraved, 18 x 11 cm. In Recueil Des Plans de L'Amerique Septentrionale Le Rouge. Paris, 1755. (Private Collection.).

1755

Braddock's Strategy, Johnson's Victory, and Cartographic Claims

Chronology

February 1755	Major General Edward Braddock arrives in Virginia and forms three-pronged strategy to contain French.

June 17	British forces seize Acadia, now Nova Scotia.
July 8	French defeat Braddock's forces near Fort Duquesne; Braddock dies.
September 9	Under the colonial general William Johnson the British win the Battle of Lake George.

I n June 1755, Baron Ludwig August Dieskau arrived in Montreal with six thousand troops to become the new military commander, but his role would be short-lived. By contrast, Pierre François de Rigaud de Vaudreuil, the Marquis de Vaudreuil (Figure 22), who arrived at the same time, to replace the Marquis Duquesne as governor of Canada, would have a major influence during the remainder of the conflict. He was the son of a previous governor of Canada and had recently served as governor of Louisiana.

In England, although war had not been declared, concern for its colonies became manifest. Major General Edward Braddock (Figure 23) was designated commander in chief of the English forces in North America and was dispatched from Ireland with two regiments. He arrived in North America in February and shortly thereafter met with the colonial governors at Alexandria, Virginia, to put forth a specific three-pronged attack to effect the rapid containment of the French. The Massachusetts regiments of Governor William Shirley and Sir William Pepperrell were to proceed to Lake Ontario, where they were to build vessels to refurbish Fort Oswego (Figure 24) and then capture Fort Niagara. Colonel William Johnson was to take Fort Frederick at Crown Point on Lake Champlain. Braddock's personal assignment was to bring about the surrender of Fort Duquesne.

Montreal

Fort Beausejour
Sackville N.B.

Fort Niagara

*Lake
Champlain*

Fort Western
Augusta

Fort Frederick
Crown Point

Fort Carillon

Lake George

Fort
William
Henry

Fort Edward

Fort Oswego
Oswego

Fort Hardy

Bay of Fundy

ACADIA
(NOVA SCOTIA)

Lake George

Fort Duquesne
Pittsburgh

Mason Dixon Line

Fort Cumberland
Cumberland

Alexandria

The war in 1755.

Figure 22.

Governor of Canada, 1755.
Pierre François de Rigaud,
the Marquis de Vaudreuil.
(Courtesy Public Archives
of Canada.)

Figure 23.

*The British
commander in chief.*
Brigadier General Edward
Braddock. (Courtesy
National Portrait Gallery,
London.)

Acadia

The first military engagement of the year, however, was not related to Braddock's plan but was directed instead at gaining possession of Acadia. Toward the end of May, Lieutenant Colonel Robert Monckton left Massachusetts with about two thousand militia for the Bay of Fundy, supported by a Captain Rous who commanded three frigates and a sloop. The English first encountered a small contingent of French troops along the shore of the Missaquash River. After gaining their surrender, they proceeded to the main French base

Figure 24.

Fort Oswego.
The South View of
Oswego, on Lake Ontario.
(Courtesy New-York
Historical Society.)

in that region, Fort Beauséjour (Figure 25). The engagement was detailed as follows on the map:

On the 1st of June, Col. Monckton arrived at Fort St. Laurence, and quartered his Troops on the Inhabitants: on the 3rd he encamped near the Fort: on the 4th he was under arms by daybreak, and at 7 o'Clock March'd with 2450 Men and 4 Field pieces, 6 Pounders.

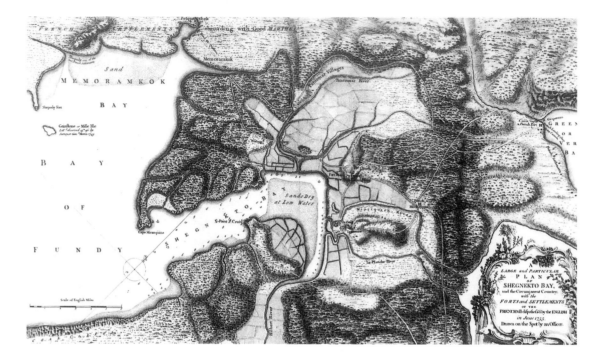

Figure 25.
Monckton's Acadia Campaign.
"A Large and Particular Plan of Shegnekto Bay and the Circumjacent Country with the Forts and Settlements of the French 'till dispossess'd by the English in June 1755. Drawn on the Spot by an Officer." Shegnekto Bay is part of the Bay of Fundy near Cape Britain. Thomas Jefferys, London, August 16, 1755. Engraving, 38 x 60cm. (Personal Collection.)

When we arrived at the carrying place over the River Missiquash, the French in the Block house (which had Cannon mounted upon it & a strong breastwork of Timber for covering the Men) fired on us: But we forc'd them to quit in an hour's time, tho' they first set fire to it, as they did, in their retreat, to all the Houses between it and the French Fort: and before Night almost all the Houses at Beausejour, to the No. of 60 were burn'd to the Ground. We were some days employ'd in clearing a Road to Transport our Cannon etc. to the place were we intended to open the Battery. On the 13th we began to fire some small Shells. On the 14th some larger; On the 15th some 16 Inch diameter; On the 16th the French Capitulated: and Terms agreed on, Col. Scot, on the 17th took possession of the Fort, and called it Fort Cumberland in honour of his Royal Highness the Duke: and the English Flag was hoisted and saluted by all the Guns on the Ramparts.

We found 24 Cannon, 12 Pounders, 1 10 Inch Mortar, and Provision for to have held out a long siege: also 150 Regular Troops and 150 Inhabitants (the remainder having escaped to Bay Verte and other distant places) who were to be sent directly by Sea to Louisbourg at our expence; and not to bear Arms for ye Space of 6 months. The Fort at Gaspreau River on Verte Bay has also surrendr'd upon Terms and Col. Winslow on the 18th took possession of it. At the attack of the Block house we had only one Man killed and Eleven wounded, one of whom is since dead; tho. they fired above 500 Shot & 60 Shells upon us yet we had not a Man hurt by either. Ensign Hay of Col. Hopson's Regiment (who was taken by the Indians in going from our Fort to the Camp & carried to the French Fort) was killed by one of our Shells as he was at breakfast with 5 French Officers, 3 of whom were also killed, and the other two wounded. Major Prebble received a slight wound in the shoulder and Ensign Tongue was wounded in the Thigh.

The French had 5 or 6 killed and have lost at the Fort 8 Officers and 51 Private Men, also 3 Indians one of whom was a Sachem of the Mickmacs.

The successful capture of Fort Beauséjour by Monckton's troops can hardly be regarded as a battle, since the English never erected a battery and the fort fell after four days of musket fire, without any direct combat between troops. On June 17th, without firing a shot, the British reduced a small fort on the Gaspereau River near a landing place on Baye Verte used as an entry point into Canada from the Atlantic Ocean. The French also abandoned

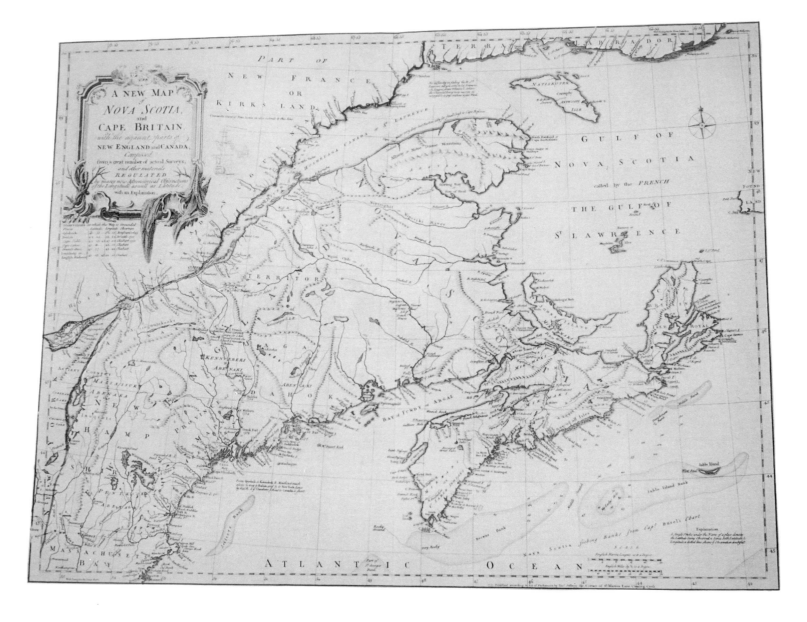

Figure 26.

Braddock Mead's Nova Scotia.
"A New Map of Nova Scotia and Cape Britain with the adjacent parts of New England and Canada, Composed from a great number of actual Surveys; and other materials Regulated by many new Astronomical Observations of the Longitude as well as Latitude; with an Explanation. Locates: Beauséjour French Fort, St. Laurence English Fort, The French Fort on Green Bay (Baye Verte) and the River Gaspero. Also On the Kennebek River; Ft. Western and Halifax built in 1754 and Frank Fort built in 1752." Engraving, 47 x 62cm, color outline by Thomas Jefferys, London. (Personal Collection.)
In the schematic representation at right, colonial names are in serif type; modern names are in sans serif type.

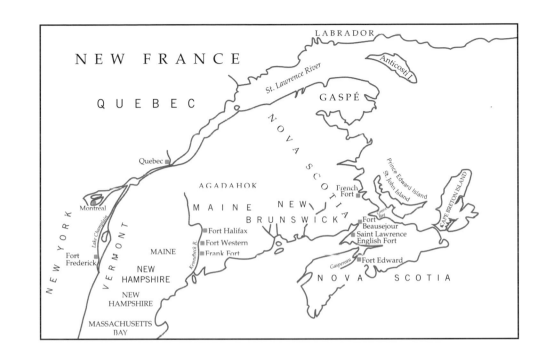

a fort on the Saint John's River. At this time the English took possession of Nova Scotia, a region the French Canadians called Acadia (Figure 26).

The year's conflict thus began with an unqualified success for the English. Governor Charles Lawrence of Nova Scotia rounded up six thousand Acadians, about half of those living in the region, and dispersed them throughout the colonies. Some found their way to New Orleans, where their descendants came to be known as Cajuns, a corrupted pronunciation of their place of origin. Those who were not dispersed escaped to Canada or islands in the Gulf of Saint Lawrence.

Braddock's March

The second and most critical battle of the year was led by Major General Braddock himself, the first British general ever to set foot in America. The object was to capture Fort Duquesne. The result was a monumental defeat that became the subject of extensive analysis.

Braddock set off for the engagement with intelligence provided by Captain Robert Stobo from his vantage point as a hostage within Fort Duquesne. Stobo suggested that one hundred Indians allied to the British might surprise the guard, which consisted of five officers and forty men, at night and thus facilitate the fort's conquest.

Braddock assembled his troops at the original Fort Cumberland in Maryland, where Wills Creek enters the Potomac, and awaited the arrival of supplies, only a fraction of which arrived. The entire force consisted of only twenty-two hundred men, including the 44th Regiment under Colonel Thomas Dunbar and the 48th under Major Sir Peter Halket, each of which had been expanded to seven hundred men with enlistments from Virginia, as well as nine companies of Virginia militia. George Washington, who according to new regulations concerning colonial officers could not serve with a rank greater than captain, elected to join the general's staff as a volunteer without rank or pay, so that he could study the art of war.

The troops got under way on June 7th for their march to Fort Duquesne, 112 miles away. Although the route was relatively straight, it passed through dense wilderness and rocky terrain, and required the creation of a road twelve feet wide. (Segments of this route would later be encompassed in the three-mile-wide survey, completed in 1768, that resulted in the Mason-Dixon Line [Figure 27]). On June 10th the troops arrived at Little Meadows with about two thousand men. At that point Braddock elected to split his force. In order to speed progress, he would himself lead about twelve hundred men and Colonel Dunbar would follow at a slower pace with eight hundred men and supplies. Washington remained with Braddock even though he was "excessively" ill recovering from the "bloody flux."

Figure 27.

The Mason-Dixon Line.
This segment of the map
shows the path of
Braddock's march. "A Plan
of the Boundary Lines
between the Province of
Maryland and the Lower
Three Counties of
Delaware with Part of the
Parallel of Pennsylvania."
[title on west section car-
touche.] Inset: "A Plan of
the West Line or parallel of
Latitude, which is the
Boundary between the
Provinces of Maryland and
Pensylvania." [Mason,
Charles and Jeremiah
Dixon.] "Dawkins, Henry
and James Smither,
engravers." Published at
Philadelphia: Robert
Kennedy, 16 August, 1768
(Personal Collection.)

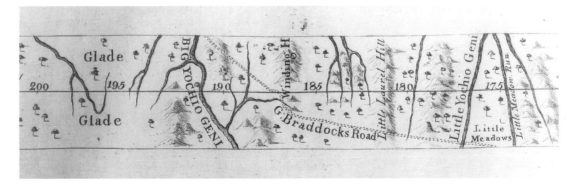

As Braddock crossed the Monongahela River below Turtle Creek, Captain Pierre de Contrecoeur, commandant of the fort, made his plans. An ambush was set at the ford of the Monongahela. The French force, led by Captain Daniel de Beaujeu, consisted of 637 Indians, 35 French officers, 72 regulars, and 146 Canadians. They were outnumbered by Braddock's 1,459 men.

On July 8th, ten miles east of Fort Duquesne, the battle took place. Contrecoeur, who was being kept informed by Indian scouts of the British advance, regarded the British position on that date to be vulnerable to an ambush. When Braddock's force was attacked, it was formed up in columns with Lieutenant Colonel Thomas Gage leading the advance guard. The French and Indians stationed themselves on the flanks of the British and shot at them from behind trees and from a vantage point on a hill. When Captain Beaujeu fell with a mortal wound early in the battle, Captain Jean Daniel Dumas took command. Braddock's vanguard, suffering significant losses, panicked and retreated to the main body, where an attitude of confusion was disseminated.

Braddock then moved out the troops he was personally leading to support Gage. There was total disarray, with British troops running in all directions. Braddock led a charge, during which his hip was shattered by a musket ball. His horse was shot from under him four times. Washington had three horses shot from under him, but although four bullets ripped through his clothing, he was not wounded.

The French losses were small—three officers killed and four wounded, with only nine regulars and Canadians killed or wounded. Braddock, mortally wounded, died four days later and was buried in an unmarked grave on the Great Meadows near the site of the abandoned Fort Necessity. Twenty-seven of eighty-nine British officers, including Sir Peter Halket and his son, and about two hundred men in the rank and file died. Nine hundred seventy-seven of the 1,459 British troops were killed or wounded; only twenty-six of the officers went unscathed.

The main force retreated rapidly to Colonel Dunbar's encampment. The entire army retrenched at Fort Cumberland, then on August 2nd left for Philadelphia. Braddock's baggage, including Captain Stobo's smuggled document (see Figure 16), fell into the hands of the French, who had few casualties. Truly surprised by their easy victory, they elected not to pursue the enemy.

When news of the bitter defeat reached London, Braddock's leadership became the subject of intense analysis and censure. The battle was chronicled in a manuscript by an anonymous participant (Figure 28) and a map that Christopher Gist drew on September 15, 1755 (Figure 29). A contemporary account, by Captain William Orme, Braddock's aide-de-camp, was accompanied by an ornate set of maps, which were published in 1768 (Figures 30 A–F). Orme presented the officers as heroes and the soldiers as culprits who evidenced "confusion," were guilty of "disobedience of orders," and exhibited "dastardly behavior." Four witnesses to the battle disagreed, leading to the conclusion that it was incompetent leadership as judged by contemporary standards, that led to the British defeat. It was argued that there was insufficient space between segments of the army, the flanking parties were inadequate to provide warning, a strategic hill along the line of march had gone unoccupied, and the main body advanced contrary to contemporary military strategies.

The Northern Theater

The second of Braddock's three proposed prongs of attack was directed against Fort Niagara. Troops led by Captain John Bradstreet reached Fort Oswego on May 27th. Before their arrival, Captain King, who commanded the one hundred men protecting the fort, received the news that forty-one French boats, each containing fifteen men, had been sighted. On June 8th a group of carpenters imported from Boston launched the first English vessel,

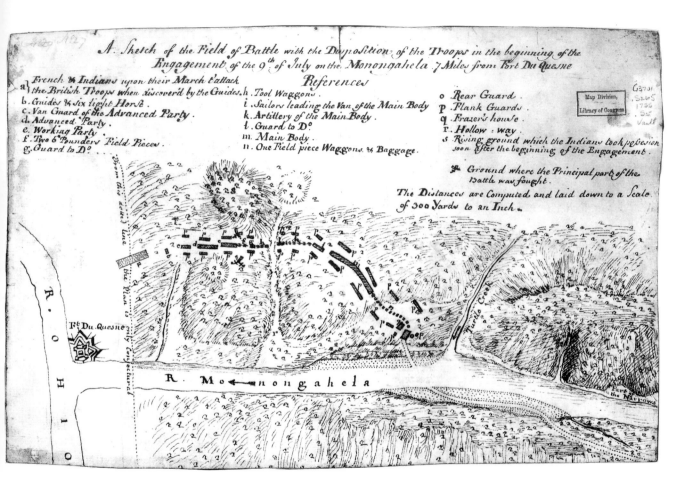

A Sketch of the Field of Battle with the Disposition of the Troops in the beginning of the Engagement of the 9th of July on the Monongahela 7 Miles from Fort Du Quesne

References

a. French & Indians upon their March t'attack the British Troops when discover'd by the Guides.
b. Guides & Six light Horse.
c. Van Guard of the Advanced Party.
d. Advanced Party.
e. Working Party.
f. Two 6 Pounders Field Pieces.
g. Guard to Do.
h. Tool Waggons.
i. Sailors leading the Van of the Main Body.
k. Artillery of the Main Body.
l. Guard to Do.
m. Main Body.
n. One Field piece Waggons & Baggage.
o. Rear Guard.
p. Flank Guards.
q. Frazer's house.
r. Hollow way.
s. Rising ground which the Indians took posession soon after the beginning of the Engagement.

☆ Ground where the Principal part of the Battle was fought.

The Distances are Computed and laid down to a Scale of 300 Yards to an Inch.

R. OHIO

Ft Du Quesne

R. Monongahela

Turtle Creek

Part of the Narrows

Figure 28.

Braddock's defense. "A Sketch of the Field of Battle with the Disposition of the Troops in the beginning of the Engagement of the 9th of July on the Monongahela 7 Miles from Fort Du Quesne." This map was probably drawn by one of Braddock's engineers. It locates the "Ground where the Principal part of the Battle was fought" as well as the point of the attack by the French and Indians, "the Guides and 6 Light Horse, the Van Guard of the Advanced Party, the Advanced Party, the Working Party, two 6 Pounders Field Pieces, the Tool Waggons, Sailors leading the Van of the Main Body, the Main Body, One Field piece Waggons &

Baggage, the Rear Guard, Flank Guards, Frazer's house, and the Rising ground which the Indians took possession soon after the beginning of the Engagement." Manuscript, 24 x 36 cm. (Courtesy Library of Congress.) Schematic representation is at right.

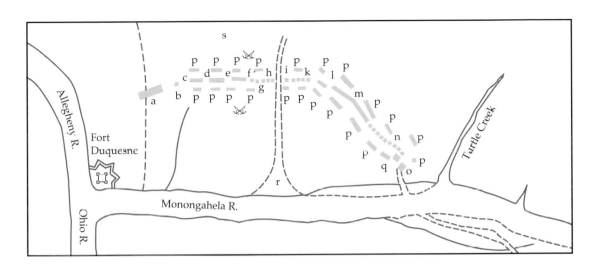

Figure 29.

Christopher Gist's map. "The Draught of Genl. Braddock's Route towards Fort DuQuesne as deliver'd to Capt. McKeller Engineer. By Christopher Gist The 15th of Sept. 1755." This map gives the distances of familiar landmarks from Fort Cumberland to Fort Duquesne, marking the camping places of the army each night. Manuscript, 35 x 46 cm. (Courtesy John Carter Brown Library.)

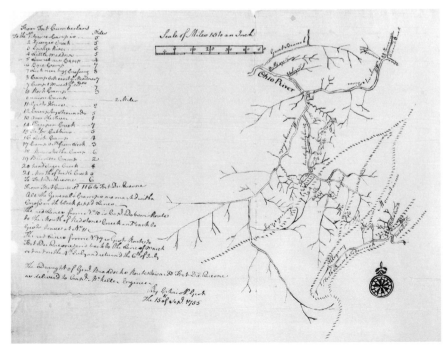

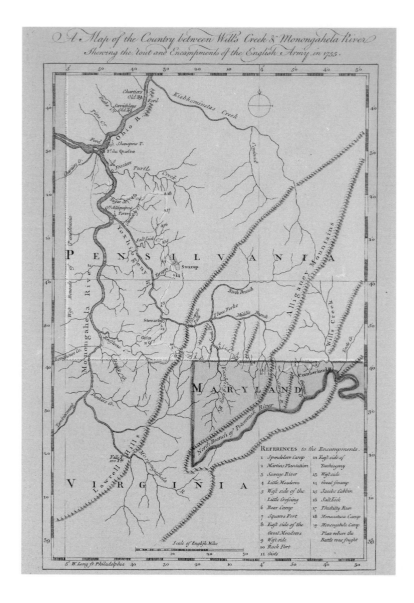

Figure 30.

The Orme maps.
Six maps by Captain William Orme, Braddock's aide-de-camp. Engravings with contemporary color and highlights. All 34 x 21 cm. From *A General Topography* by Thomas Jefferys. London, 1768. (Personal Collection.)

Figure 30A.

"A Map of the Country between Will's Creek & Monongahela River Showing the Rout and Encampments of the English Army in 1755." The map contains numbered references to the (1) Spendelon Camp; (2) Martins Plantation; (3) Savage River; (4) Little Meadows; (5) West side of the Little Crossing; (6) Bear camp; (7) Squares Fort; (8) East side of the Great Meadows; (9) West side; (10) Rock Fort; (11) Gists; (12) East side of Yaxhiogeny; (13) West side; (14) Great Swamp; (15) Jacobs Cabbin; (16) Salt Lick; (17) Thickitty Run; (18) Monacatuca Camp; (19) Monongahela Camp; and "Place where the Battle was fought."

Figure 30B.

"A Plan of the Line of March with the whole Baggage." The column was led by a "Corporal with Light Horse" followed by a "Serjeant with Carpenters," an "Officer and 19 Light Horse, A company of Carpenters & 15 Seamen, A Tumbril with Tools, 2 Field Pieces, Van Guard and a Field Officer, Grenadier Company and Sir Peter Halkett" in a row, followed by two parallel columns, staggering the components of each column. On the left were the "Col's. Company, 2nd Captain, 5th Captain, 1st Captain, 2d Grenadier Company, a Field Officer, Capt. Dagworthy at the head of Maryland Comp, Captain Rutherford at the head of Independents, Captain Hogg and the Virginia Rangers, Captain Stephens and the Virginia Rangers." On the right were "Major's Company, 4th Captain, 3d Captain, Lt. Col's Company, Captain Waggoner and Virginia Rangers, Captain Gates and Independents, Captain Dobbs and Independents, Capt. Cook's Virginia Rangers and the 2d Field Officer." Bringing up the rear were "Colonel Dunbar, Provost General and Women, 2d Company of Grenadiers, 2 Field Pieces, 1st Company of Grenadiers, a Corporal and 4 Light Horses."

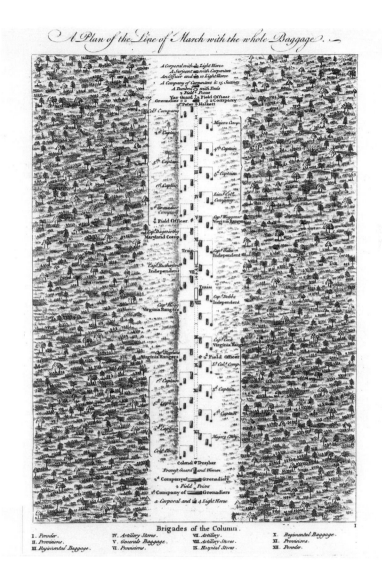

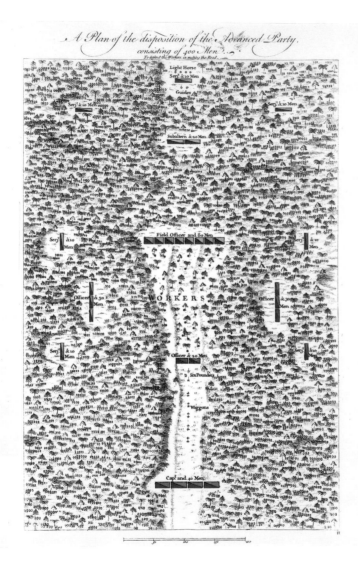

Figure 30C.

"A Plan of the disposition of the Advanced Party, consisting of 400 Men. To defend the Workers in making the Road." In the front are "Light Horse Serjt. & 10 Men and Guides" followed by "Subaltern & 20 Men, Field Officer and 80 Men." Workers are in the center, followed by "Officer & 20 Men, Six Pounders, Waggons, Capt. & 40 Men." On the flanks are "Serjt. & 10 Men, Serjt. & 10 Men, Officer & 30 Men, Serjt. & 10 Men." 34 x 21 cm.

Figure 30D.

"A Plan of the Line of March of the Detachment from the little Meadows. The column is led by "Light Horse," followed by "30 Sailors, Detacht, 1 Subaltern & 20 Grenadiers, a 12 pounder, Company of Grenadiers, Van Guard, Subaltern & 20 Men, Subaltern & 20 Men; Train, Centre, Sir Peter Halkets and Centre, Col Dunbars; in parallel, Train, Two Subalterns each with 10 Men, 12 pounder, Company of Grenadiers, Subaltern & 20 Men, and Light Horse." On each flank are "two Light Horse, Five Serjt. each with 10 Men," and "Three Subalterns each with 20 Men."

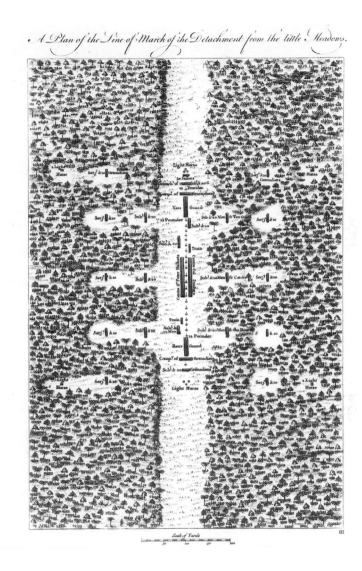

A Plan of the Line of March of the Detachment from the little Meadows.

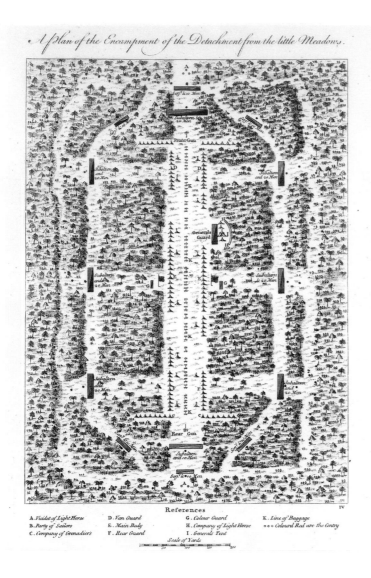

A Plan of the Encampment of the Detachment from the little Meadows.

References

A . Viudet of Light Horse   D . Van Guard   G . Colour Guard   K . Line of Baggage
B . Party of Sailors   E . Main Body   H . Company of Light Horse   ○○○ Colourd Red are the Centry
C . Company of Grenadiers   F . Rear Guard   I . Generals Tent

Scale of Yards

Figure 30E.

"A Plan of the Encampment of the Detachment from the little Meadows." At the front and rear are "Viudets of Light Horse." The outer circle is made up of "six groups of Serjt. each with 10 Men, eight groups of 20 Men each commanded by a Subaltern." In the center there is a "Front Gun and a Rear Gun, a Party of Sailors, Company of Grenadiers, Van Guard, Main Body, Rear Guard, Colour Guard, Company of Light Horse, General's Tent, and Line of Baggage." Sentries are posted around the encampment in the woods.

Figure 30F.

"A Plan of the Field of Battle and disposition of the Troops, as they were on the March at the Time of the Attack on the 9th of July 1755." The battlefield is flanked by the Ohio River to the north, the Monongahela to the west, and Turtle Creek to the south. Frazer's House and Fort Duquesne are here computed to be seven miles apart. The position of the French and Indians when discovered by the guides is shown. Letters designate the location of (a) Guides with 6 Light Horse; (b) Van of the advanced party; (c) Advanced party of 350 Men commanded by Lt. Col. Gage; (d)Working party of 250 Men commanded by Sir John St. Clair; (e) Five Field Pieces, 6 Pounders; (f) Guard; (g) Tool Waggons; (h) Flank Guards and Main Body of Army; (i) Light Horse; (k) Sailors; (l) Serjeants & 10 Grenadiers; (m) Subalterns & 20 Men; (n) 12 Pounders; (o) Company of Grenadiers; (p) Van Guard; (q) Train of Artillery; (r) Sir Peter Halkets; (s) Col. Dunbar's; (t) Rear Guard; (u) A Mill; (w) Ground where the principal part of the Engagement was fought.

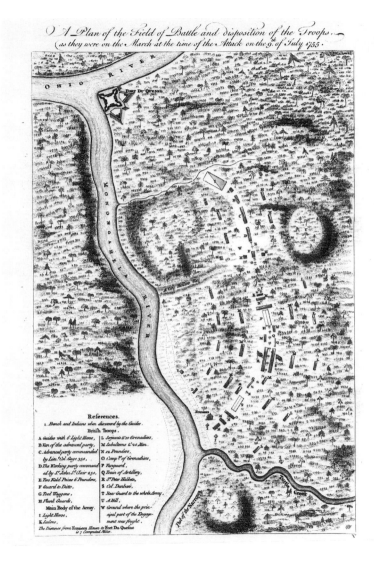

the *Oswego*, on Lake Ontario (Figure 31). In early July Sir William Pepperrell's Jersey Blues, commanded by Colonel Philip Schuyler, began their march to the fort, but news of Braddock's defeat led to many desertions. Toward the end of July, General William Shirley left Albany (Figure 32) and reached Oswego (see Figure 24) on August 18th. In September he elected to defer the attack on Fort Niagara until the following year. Seven hundred men under Lieutenant Colonel Hugh Mercer were left to secure the post at Oswego and build two new forts in the region. The fleet—which by that time had been expanded to include a decked sloop with eight four-pounders and thirty swivels and two undecked schooners with swivels—was unrigged and laid up. The French were left with a distinct advantage on the lake.

The Crown Point Campaign

The last of the proposals put forth by Braddock at the strategic council in Alexandria, Virginia, namely to attack Crown Point on Lake Champlain, resulted in a surprising success and the emergence of the first major hero of the war: William Johnson, an Irish immigrant who became the most influential Indian leader in North America and for whom Fort Johnson was named (Figure 33). In April 1755 he was promoted to major general and assigned the role of leadership for the proposed attack on Fort Frederick (Crown Point), located on the western shore of Lake Champlain (Figure 34). Massachusetts, Connecticut, New Hampshire, Rhode Island, and New York raised a total of four thousand men to serve under his command. Included in the New Hampshire contingent was twenty-three-year-old Captain Robert Rogers, who would gain fame as the leader of his Rangers (Figure 35).

In the middle of July the first division was led up the Hudson River by Johnson's second in command, Colonel G. Phineas Lyman. At Saratoga, on the north side of Fish Creek they built a blockhouse that became Fort Hardy (Figure 36), and a storehouse built at a

Figure 31.

Lake Ontario.
"Lake Ontario to the Mouth of the River St. Lawrence," showing Fort Ontario and Oswego, Fort Niagara, and Fort Frontenac. Engraved by T. Kitchin. 23 x 25 cm. In *The History of the Late War in North-America*, by Thomas Mante. London, 1772. (Personal Collection.)

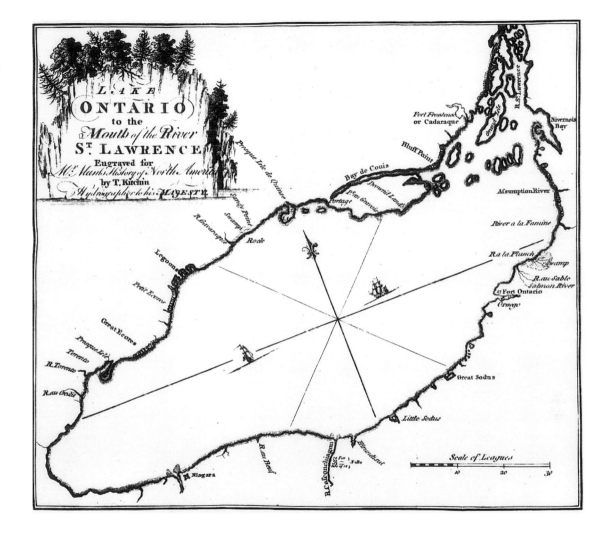

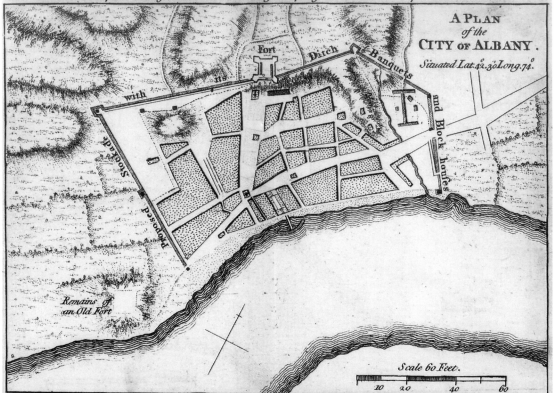

With a Design for the better securing it by altering the ancient form of its Stockade adding a Ditch in Front defended by a Number of Block houses with a Banquette within, from which a double Fire of Musquetry can be Made thro loop holes in the Stockade.

A PLAN of the CITY of ALBANY.
Situated Lat. 42.30 Long. 74.0

Also a Design for a Magazine for Provisions, Barracks for to Compleat 1000 Men with a General Hospital for 400 Sick and a small Quay for the Conveniency of Loading & Unloading the Vessels which will also serve for a Battery for 2 Guns to Command the River

Figure 32.

Albany, New York.
"A Plan of the City of Albany. With a Design for the better securing it by altering the ancient form of its Stockade adding a Ditch in Front defended by a Number of Block houses with a Banquette within from which a double Fire of Musquetry can be Made through loop holes in the Stockade. Also a Design for a Magazine for Provisions, Barracks for to Compleat 1000 Men with a General Hospital for 400 Sick and a small Quay for the Conveniencing of Loading & Unloading the Vessels which will also serve for a Battery for 2 Guns to Command the River." Engraved, 12 x 17cm. In *A Set of Plans and Forts in America*. London: [John Rocque], 1763. (Personal Collection.)

Figure 33.

Fort Johnson.
Previously known as
Mount Johnson, the fort
was drawn before 1759
by Sir William Johnson's
nephew and son-in-law,
Guy Johnson. (Courtesy
New York Public Library.)

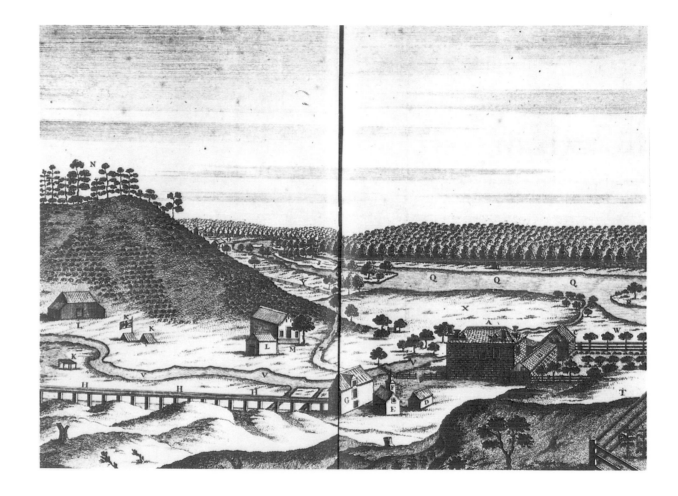

carrying place (portage) was named Fort Miller. Below the falls of the Hudson at a strategic portage between the Hudson River and Lac Saint Sacrement they built a log fort, which for diplomatic reasons Johnson had christened Fort Lyman, to honor his associate. Shortly thereafter it was renamed Fort Edward (Figure 37), honoring one of the king's grandsons.

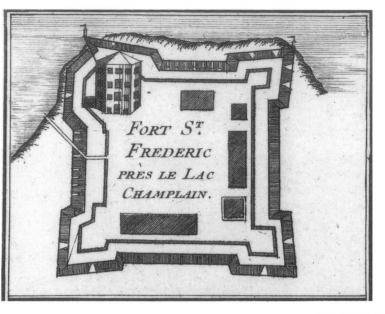

Johnson was joined by his old Indian compatriot Hendrick, the Mohawk sachem, and in mid-August with about two thousand men he proceeded to the southern shore of Lac Saint Sacrement, to which Johnson assigned the name Lake George, "not only to honor his Majesty but to ascertain his undoubted dominion here." Johnson intended to sail down Lake George to Ticonderoga on the western shore of the narrows connecting Lake George with Lake Champlain, then proceed north to assault Crown Point. He initially selected a campsite abutting the southern shore of Lake George and ordered Captain William Eyre to direct the construction of Fort William Henry to protect the area.

Meanwhile, the French commander in chief, Marshal Ludwig August Dieskau, had arrived at Crown Point with a force of 3,573 men, including regulars,

Figure 34.

Crown Point. "Fort St. Frederic près de Lac Champlain." Engraved, 8 x 19 cm. In *Recueil des Plans de l'Amérique Septentrionale.* Le Rouge, Paris, 1755. (Personal Collection.)

Figure 35.

Robert Rogers. Twenty-three-year-old future leader of Rogers' Rangers. (Courtesy New Hampshire Historical Society.)

Figure 36.

Fort Hardy (Saratoga).
"A Plan of the Fort at Saratoga." Engraved, 12 x 17 cm. In *A Set of Plans and Forts in America. Reduced from Actual Surveys.* London: [John Rocque], 1763. (Personal Collection.)

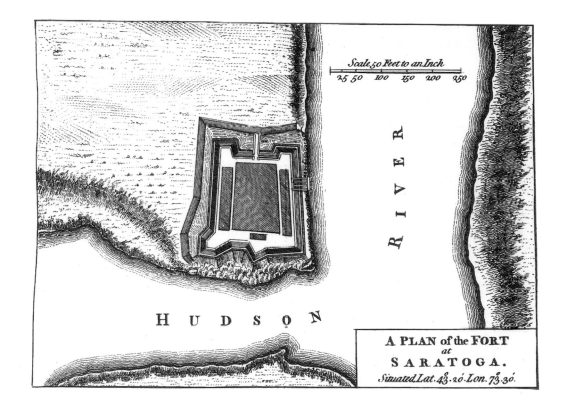

Canadians, and Indians. The French had been made aware of the British plans when they had captured Braddock's war chest. Fort Frederick was reinforced with seven hundred men and the remaining force proceeded to the promontory at Ticonderoga. Dieskau ordered that a fort be built at that point, upon which the engineer, Captain Lotbinière, named it Fort Carillon, for the sounds made by the water striking the rocks and the wind passing through the trees.

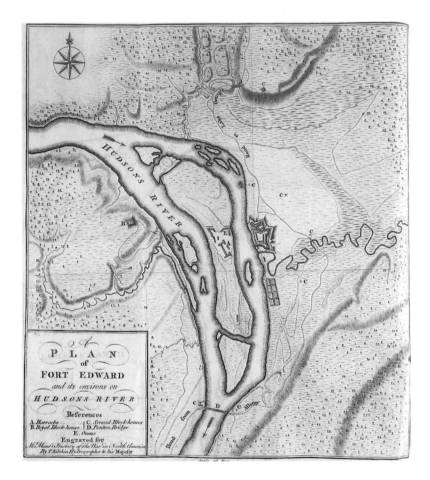

Figure 37A.

Fort Edward.
"A Plan of Fort Edward
and its environs on
Hudsons River." Engraved
by T. Kitchin in *The History
of the Late War in North
America* by Thomas Mante.
London, 1772. 29 x 26 cm.
References: (a) Barracks;
(b) Royal Block house; (c)
Several Block houses; (d)
Pontoon Bridge; (e) Ovens.

Fort Edward.
"Plan of Fort Edward."
Engraved, 12 x 17 cm. In
*A Set of Plans and Forts in
America. Reduced from
Actual Surveys.* London:
[John Rocque], 1763.

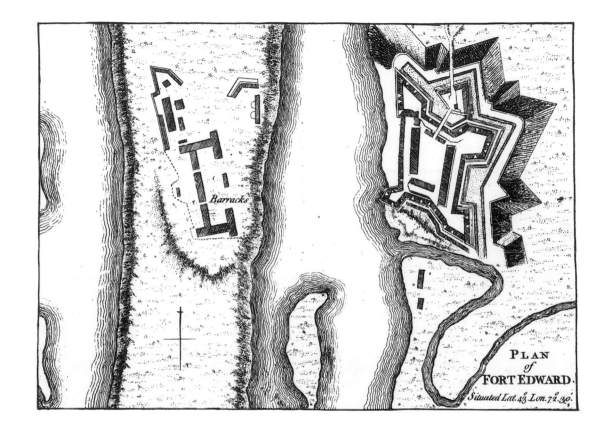

PLAN
of
FORT EDWARD.
Situated Lat. 43. Lon. 72.30.

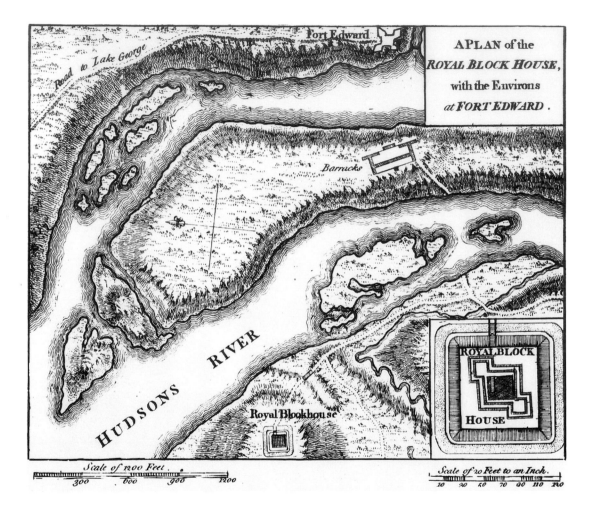

Labels within the map: Fort Edward · Road to Lake George · A PLAN of the ROYAL BLOCK HOUSE, with the Environs at FORT EDWARD. · Barracks · HUDSONS RIVER · Royal Blockhouse · ROYAL BLOCK HOUSE · Scale of 1200 Feet. 300 600 900 1200 · Scale of 20 Feet to an Inch. 10 20 50 70 90 110 130

Figure 37C.

The Blockhouse.
"A Plan of the Royal Block House, with the Environs at Fort Edward." Engraved, 12 x 17 cm. In *A Set of Plans and Forts in America. Reduced from Actual Surveys.* London: [John Rocque], 1763. (Personal Collection.)

On September 5th, Dieskau, with two hundred regulars, six hundred Canadians, and six hundred Indians, sailed to the head of the bay and up Wood Creek. The following day they began their march toward Fort Lyman (Fort Edward). The French penetrated to within a few miles of the fort. When they were informed by a prisoner that the main encampment was along the southern shore of Lake George they diverged toward that target.

Having learned of the presence of the French, Johnson sent two hundred Indians under Hendrick and troops led by Colonel Ephraim Williams to confront the French.

On September 8th the first phase of battle, known as the Bloody Morning Scout, took place at Rocky Brook. Dieskau, notified of the English advance, deployed the Indians into the woods so they could attack from the rear. The Canadians would attack from the flanks, while the regulars were to await the English front. The English, under Williams, accompanied by their Indian comrades, marched with a force of five hundred men into a trap leading to the death of many, including Hendrick and Williams. (On July 22nd, in Albany, Williams had made a will that was to provide funds for the establishment of a men's college in western Massachusetts. Thus Williams College had its origin.) In the same engagement, Jacques Legardeur de Saint Pierre, the recipient of the letter George Washington had carried to Fort Le Beouf in 1753, was also killed. The English retreated to their encampment, where a breastwork of trees and overturned wagons had been built to deter the advancement of the French.

Dieskau then led a joint French, Canadian, and Indian advance against Johnson and the main English force. Johnson, rallying his troops, positioned 250 men on each flank extending from the camp to the lake, with the remaining troops placed in front of the camp facing the road. The French attacked in three straight lines with bayonets fixed. The first row fired in unison, then moved to the rear. The second and third rows followed in similar fashion, advancing slowly each time. This maneuver had little effect on the British. A French assault of the breastwork also failed, at which point the British counterattacked, climbing over the breastworks and putting the French forces to flight. Dieskau, wounded, was taken prisoner and ultimately shipped to England. More than 260 French forces were killed. The remaining French troops retreated in disarray to Crown Point. Johnson, who had taken a bullet in a leg, had led a colonial army unfortified by British professionals and repulsed a trained command of French regulars, Canadians, and Indians for the first time in the century. This feat, which would not be repeated for another three years, earned William Johnson a baronetcy and a gift of £5,000.

The first two phases of the battle of Lake George are depicted in a representation by Samuel Blodget, the first print of a battle on the North American continent to be published in America (Figure 38).

The battle actually had a third phase. Colonel Joseph Blanchard, at Fort Lyman, heard the shooting and sent a detachment of 250 men to assist Johnson's troops. They arrived after the battle had ended but, coming upon a group of Canadians and Indians at Rocky Brook, attacked and defeated them, killing a large number. This led to the name Bloody Pond being assigned to the pool from which the brook ran. Throughout all three phases the French lost about 400 men and the provincials 262, plus officers and 38 Indians.

After the battle, Johnson directed that Fort William Henry, named for another of the king's grandsons, be completed at the site of the encampment on the south shore of Lake George (Figure 39). On September 24th, Captain Robert Rogers of New Hampshire was sent to Crown Point, where he found five thousand French troops erecting batteries. Then on October 7th he proceeded to Ticonderoga, where he noted two thousand of the French laying a foundation for a fort to command the pass between Lakes George and Champlain. Realizing from this information that an attack on the fort was impractical, Johnson left Captain Rogers in charge of Forts William Henry and Edward, and Johnson left for Albany.

At about this time, Governor-General William Shirley was initiating the campaign against Fort Niagara. In early August, Shirley led troops from Albany to Schenectady (Figure 40), and then in bateaux up the Mohawk River to the portage known as the Great Carrying Place (see Figure 48). Here he learned of Braddock's defeat and the death of his son William Shirley. They then traveled by boat across Lake Oneida and north up the

Figure 38.

The Battle of Lake George. "A Prospective Plan of the Battle Fought near Lake George on the 8th of September 1755, between 2000 English with 250 Mohawks under the Command of General Johnson and 2500 French and Indians under the Command of General Dieskau in which the English were victorious, captivating the French General with a Number of his Men, killing 700 and putting the rest to flight. S. Blodget Del. and Thos. Johnston Sculp." Engraved, 35 x 45cm. Boston, 1755. (Courtesy Colonial Williamsburg, Virginia.)

The plan is in two parts. To the left is the first engagement, with five reference numbers; to the right is the second engagement, with reference numbers 6 through 39, explained in an accompanying pamphlet. There are also insets of "Hudsons River," Fort Edward, and Fort William Henry.

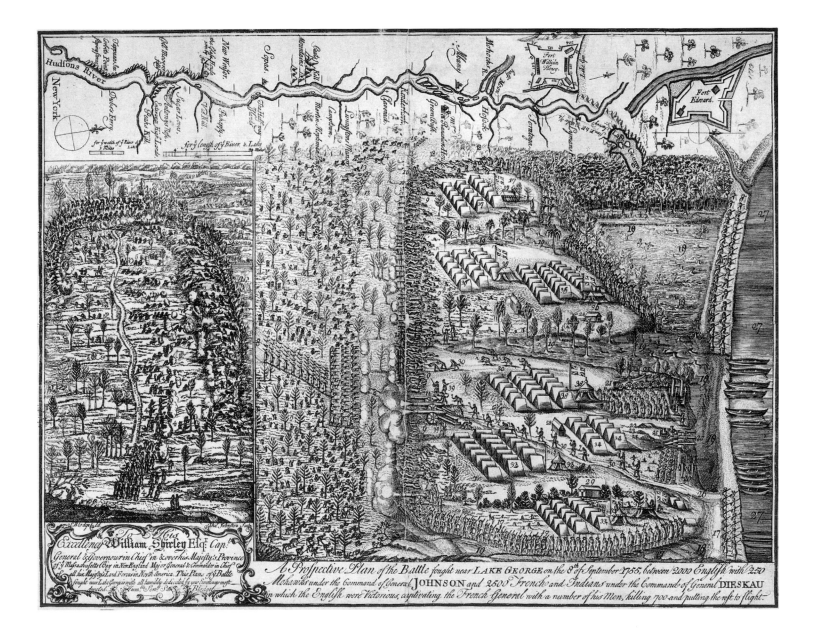

Onondaga River to where it emptied into Lake Ontario. There they reached their destination, Fort Oswego. The first English warship of the Lake Ontario fleet, christened the *Oswego*, had just been completed. Her sister ship the *Ontario* would soon be ready.

In the fall of the year, there was still no firm or cohesive commitment by the colonies. By mid-October five hundred Virginia militiamen were sent to Fort Cumberland. In Pennsylvania, the governor initially failed to raise troops, but when Indians drove provincial inhabitants out of Tulpekochen and survivors began arriving at the state house with dead bodies, the Quakers agreed to provide monies to outfit a militia.

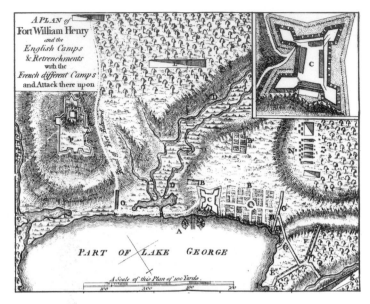

Figure 39A.

Fort William Henry. "A Plan of Fort Henry and the English Camps & Retrenchments with the French different Camps and Attack there upon. Engraved, 12 x 17 cm. In *A Set of Plans and Forts in America. Reduced from Actual Surveys.* London: [John Rocque], 1763. (Personal Collection.).

Keyed to (A) The Dock; (B) The Garrison Gardens; (C) Fort William Henry; (D) The Different Morass; (E) The Enemy's Battery of 9 Guns & 2 Mortars; (F) Their 2d Battery of 10 Guns and 3 Mortars; (G) Their Approaches; (H) Two Intended Batterys; (I) The Place where they landed their Artillery; (K) Mr. Montcalm's Camp with the main Body of ye Army; (L) Mr. de Levis Camp with 4000

Critical Maps of 1755

The year 1755 saw the publication of several important maps that asserted boundaries and made graphic statements of claims. The geography of the distant continent with its burgeoning colonies and contested lands was now depicted for the interested English and European citizenry. Descriptive annotations often provided a specific historical basis for nations' claims, and the positions of both protective and threatening fortifications were defined.

Regulars & Canadians; (M) Mr. de la Corne with 1500 Canadians & Indians; (N) The Ground where the English Troops Encamped before they was ordered by Gl. Wiod to the Place where the Retrenchment was made; (O) The bridge over ye Morass; (P) The English Retrenchment.

Figure 39B.

Fort William Henry. Engraved, 12 x 17 cm. In *A Set of Plans and Forts in America. Reduced from Actual Surveys.* London: [John Rocque], 1763. (Personal Collection.)

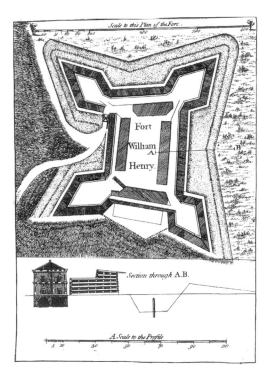

The first and most famous of these maps was made by John Mitchell and published in London on February 13, 1755. The Lords Commissioners of Trade and Plantations retained Mitchell, a Virginia-born physician who emigrated to England, to redraw and improve a map he had executed in 1750. They gave an order for each colonial governor to provide a map or chart of his province. The first (1755) edition was entitled "A Map of the British and French Dominions in North America with the Roads, Distances, Limits, and Extent of the Settlements…" (Figure 41. See plate 1). The title of the fourth edition was changed to "A Map of the British Colonies in North America with the Roads, Distances, Limits, and Extent of the Settlements…" The map, which was five years in preparation, bears the endorsement of John Pownall, Secretary of the Lords Commissioners (Figure 42. See plate 2). The large (132 x 191 cm) map identifies cities, towns, villages, forts and fortifications, Indian towns and villages and deserted settlements, rivers and falls, roads and distances. This frankly political map depicts the division of the eastern portion of North America between the British and the French. The boundaries of the English colonies extend westward across the Mississippi River to the western border of the map reflecting their "sea to sea" charters. In support of the British claims, the dates of the victories that led to British annexations of land appear, and areas previously surrendered by the French are specified.

In 1755, Thomas Jefferys, in London, published Braddock Mead's map of Nova Scotia (see Figure 26), accompanying it with a pamphlet denouncing the French. Jefferys followed by reprinting a French map of Cape Breton and an English one of Nova Scotia, one above the other, each showing its own claims. On November 29th, 1755, Jefferys also published Mead's map "A Most Inhabited Part of New England containing the Provinces of Massachusetts Bay and New Hampshire with the Colonies of Kenektikut and Rhode Island. The first edition of this map measures 98 x 104 cm and has an inset plan entitled "Fort Frederick, A French encroachment, built 1731 at Crown Point."

The use of maps to make political statements is most blatantly evident in "A New and Accurate Map of the English Empire in North America: Representing their Rightful Claim as confirm'd by Charters, and the formal Surrender of their Indian Friends; Likewise the Encroachments of the French with the several Forts they have unjustly erected therein. By a Society of Anti-Gallicans." This map, published in London in December 1755 by William Herbert and Robert Sayer, contains seven insets focusing on French forts, towns, and harbors (Figure 43. See plates 4 and 5). On the map, the society claimed that England had already won the war.

In that same year, Thomas Bowen and John Gibson produced a large wall map titled "An Accurate Map of North America . . . Exhibiting the Present Seat of War and the French Encroachments." Also, John Huske borrowed features from the Mitchell map to accompany his emotional, patriotic dissertation called "The Present State of North America." This map (Figure 44. See plate 3), "A New and Accurate Map of North America (where in all the Errors of all preceding British, French and Dutch maps respecting the rights of Great Britain, France & Spain, & Limits of each of His Majesty's Provinces, are corrected)," depicts British claims extending to the western limits of the chart. The map claims that the western boundary of Acadia is the Saint Croix River. It notes that the land of the Iroquois or Five Nations has been ceded by many treaties and sales by the Indians as well as the

Figure 40.

Schenectady.
"A Plan of Schenectady." Engraved, 12 x 17 cm. In *A Set of Plans and Forts in America. Reduced from Actual Surveys.* London: [John Rocque], 1763. (Personal Collection.)

References: "(A) Schenectady; (B) Wooden fort with four Block houses for flankers; (C) Block houses to defend the Stockades; (D) Stockades planted around the Town; (E) The Nearest high Ground to ye Town which is about 600 yds. from ye Stockades; (F) Part of a line of an Encampment thrown up and a facine Battery to shew how such works are Constructed; (G) Barracks or Sheds where part of ye Regt. were lodged last Winter. The Boundary on each side of the River is pretty nearly on a Level except where it's marked otherwise on the Draught."

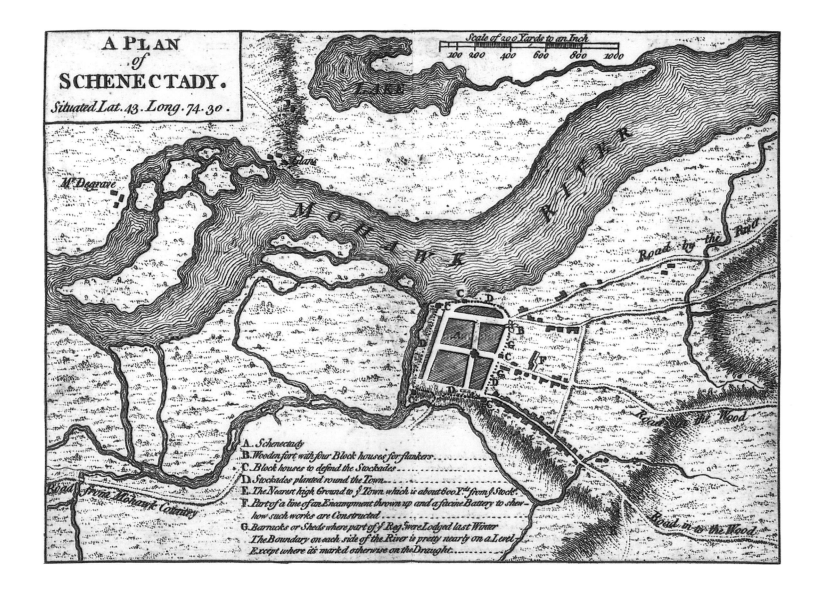

A PLAN
of
SCHENECTADY.

Situated Lat. 43. Long. 74. 30.

Scale of 200 Yards to an Inch
100 200 400 600 800 1000

LAKE

MOHAWK RIVER

Mr Degrave

Island

Road by the River

C
C C D B
C
D C
E F
C
D D
A C
D
C

Road in the Wood

Road from Mohawk Country

Road in the Wood

A. Schenectady
B. Wooden fort with four Block houses for flankers ....
C. Block houses to defend the Stockades ....
D. Stockades planted round the Town ....
E. The Nearest high Ground to ye Town which is about 800 Yd from ye Stock.
F. Part of a line of an Encampment thrown up and a facine Battery to shew ---
   how such works are Constructed ....
G. Barracks or Sheds where part of ye Reg ¦ were Lodged last Winter
   The Boundary on each side of the River is pretty nearly on a Level ----
   Except where its mark'd otherwise on the Draught. ....

French in the Treaties of Utrecht and Aix-la-Chapelle. This vast expanse extends some twelve hundred miles north-south and eight hundred miles east-west. Similar to the presentation of the so designated Anti-Gallican map, colored portions of the Huske map delineate land claimed by Great Britain, with an uncolored area north of the Saint Lawrence River presented as all France can claim. An uncolored portion south of Georgia is regarded as belonging to Spain.

In 1755, France countered cartographically with maps by d'Anville, Robert de Vaugondy, and Bellin. Jean Baptiste Bourguignon d'Anville's "Canada Louisiane et Terres Angloises" extends from the northern tip of Newfoundland to northern Florida and depicts Lake Michigan with an incorrect southwesterly tilt, to place more land within the French area. The borders of Carolina and Virginia stop at the Montanes Bleues (Allegheny Mountains). Forts Duquesne, Detroit, and Le Boeuf are identified. There is also a large inset of the main highway of New France, Le Fleuve Saint-Laurent (Figure 45. See plate 6).

The map titled "Partie Occidentale de la Nouvelle France ou Canada," by Jacques Nicolas Bellin, specifically places the western English boundary east of Lake Champlain and along the summit of the Appalachian Mountains. It locates Fort Duquesne and the "place of a previous English fort [Fort Prince George] in that region" (Figure 46. See plate 7).

The perspective of the English colonists in 1755 was expressed by Lewis Evans in a map published that year in Philadelphia and London. His "A General Map of the Middle British Colonies, in America…" is considered one of the landmarks of American cartography. It depicts an area from Montreal and the lower end of Lake Huron to the North Carolina border, from the Atlantic coast to the "land of the Welinis corrupted to Ilinois." It locates Forts Duquesne, Detroit, and Niagara. An inset emphasizes the importance of the Ohio Valley in the struggle for supremacy against the French (Figure 47. See plate 8). In an accompanying analysis printed by Benjamin Franklin and David Hall, Evans states that the "very valuable country on the Ohio is now the Object of British and French policy."

5

1756

French Advances

Chronology

March 1	Louis-Joseph de Montcalm appointed commander in chief of French forces in North America.
March 17	Earl of Loudoun appointed commander in chief of British forces.
May 18–19	Great Britain declares war on France; France reciprocates.

| August 14 | French under Montcalm capture Fort Oswego |
| December | Montcalm winters in Montreal and Quebec, the English in New York, Boston, and Philadelphia. |

T he year 1756 saw a formal declaration of war between Great Britain and France and a change in the leadership on both sides in North America. The British court increased the efforts in North America in response to pleas from the provinces, building a string of forts between Albany and Lake Ontario (Figure 48). In February, Fort Williams was completed on the bank of the Mohawk River at the Great Carry Place portage between that river and Wood Creek. Fort Bull was built four miles to the west, near Wood Creek. A blockhouse was built on the east end of Lake Oneida (Figure 49), and the area around Nicholas Herkimer's house at German Flats was retrenched (Figure 50). These forts were all positioned to maintain access to the Great Lakes.

Lieutenant General Louis-Joseph de Montcalm-Gozon, marquis de Montcalm de Saint-Véran (Figure 51) was appointed supreme commander of the French on March 1st and arrived in Canada in May. He would encounter two enemies during the remainder of his heroic career, the British forces and Governor Pierre de Rigaud, the marquis Vaudreuil, who was openly antagonistic to Montcalm and plotted against him in his communiqués to France.

John Campbell, the fourth earl of Loudoun, received his commission as commander in chief of the British troops on March 17th, although he had actually been appointed in January. He did not leave for America until May 20th and did not arrive until July 22nd. On May 18th, two days before Loudoun's departure and almost two years to the day that

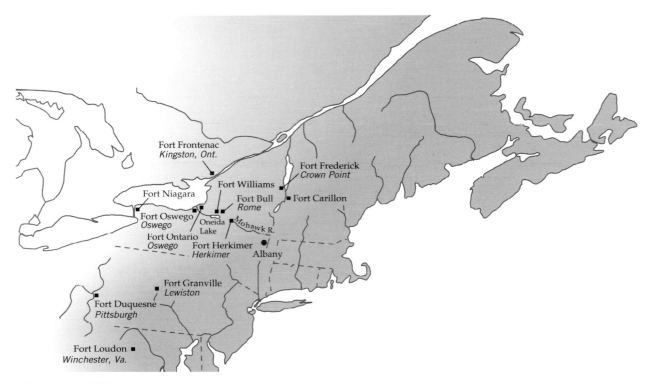

Fort Frontenac
Kingston, Ont.

Fort Frederick
Crown Point

Fort Williams

Fort Niagara

Fort Bull
Rome

Fort Carillon

Fort Oswego
Oswego

Oneida
Lake

Mohawk R.

Fort Ontario
Oswego

Fort Herkimer
Herkimer

Albany

Fort Granville
Lewiston

Fort Duquesne
Pittsburgh

Fort Loudon
Winchester, Va.

The war in 1756.

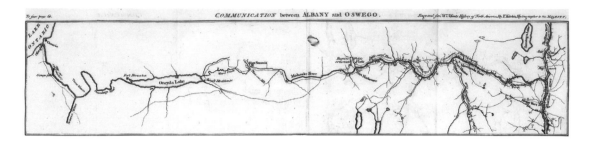

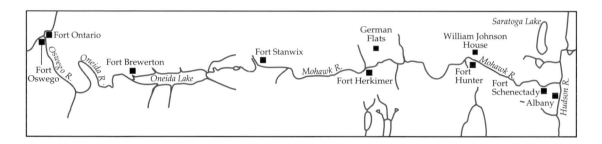

Figure 48.

British forts in New York. "Communication between Albany and Oswego." T. Kitchin. Engraved, black and white. 13 x 59 cm. In *The History of the Late War in North America*, by Thomas Mante. London: 1772. (Personal Collection.) Schematic representation is below the map.

George Washington started the shooting, Great Britain declared war on France. The next day, France responded with a similar declaration.

In March, William Shirley of Massachusetts moved to reinforce Fort Oswego and placed Lieutenant Colonel John Bradstreet in charge of the effort. The French had already set out to cut off supplies to the fort and had dispatched 360 French troops, along with Canadians and Indians under Lieutenant Claude de Léry to attack Fort Bull. Three

Figure 49.

The Oneida blockhouse. "Scetch of the Blockhouse at the East of Oneida Lake." Engraved, black and white. 12 x 17 cm. In *A Set of Plans and Forts in America. Reduced from Actual Surveys.* London: [John Rocque], 1763. (Personal Collection.)

Figure 50.

German Flats. "Plan and Profile of Retrenched Work round Herkimer's house at ye German Flats 1756." Engraved, 12 x 17 cm. In *A Set of Plans and Forts in America. Reduced from Actual Surveys.* London: [John Rocque], 1763. (Personal Collection.)

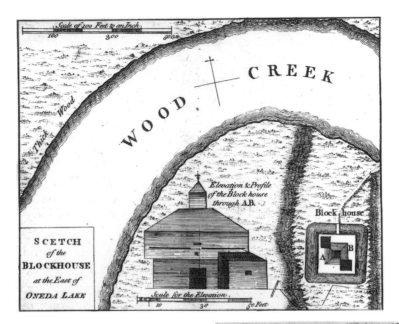

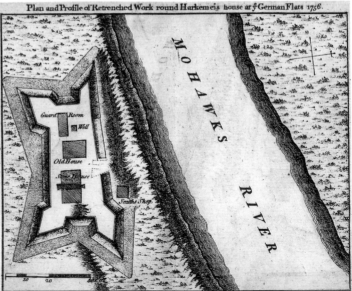

wagons with twelve soldiers that left the fort were ambushed. The fort's portal was smashed in and all but two of the two dozen soldiers within slaughtered. The French destroyed the fort along with provisions for Fort Oswego's relief.

Bradstreet then built one hundred new boats and delivered food and goods to the fort from Albany, traveling a distance of 160 miles to do so. He and his troops were ambushed by the French on their return trip, but his outnumbered force routed their attackers. This constituted the last good news Albany would receive for two years, at which time Bradstreet would triumph again.

The French put into effect their plan to capture Fort Oswego as soon as the Saint Lawrence River became navigable. Thirteen hundred regulars, seventeen hundred militiamen, and many Indians assembled at Fort Frontenac (Figure 52) were joined by Montcalm on July 29th. Two armed vessels were positioned in Lake Ontario opposite the fort. By August 12th the French troops were in place outside Fort Ontario (Figure 53) and the English retreated. The British forces within Fort Oswego had been badly neglected and were demoralized at the time they were confronted with the siege. When a scout reported the presence of French boats on Lake Ontario, Colonel Hugh Mercer, Fort Oswego's commandant, ordered an attack by the crew of the *Oswego*. Then, assessing the impossibility of

Figure 51.

The Marquis de Montcalm. Louis-Joseph de Montcalm-Gozon, the marquis de Montcalm de Saint-Véran. (Courtesy Public Archives of Canada.)

Figure 52.

Fort Frontenac.
"Plan of Fort Frontenac."
Engraved, 12 x 17 cm. In
*A Set of Plans and Forts in
America. Reduced from
Actual Surveys.* London:
[John Rocque], 1763.
(Personal Collection.)

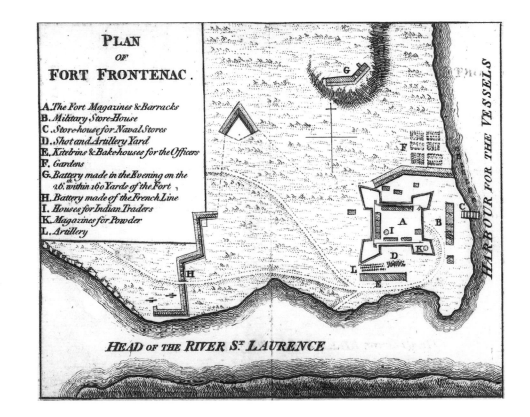

defending the fort, he ordered its guns spiked and had some of the garrison retreat by boat.
The bombardment began on August 14th. Mercer was killed by a cannon shot, and it was
left for Lieutenant Colonel John Littlehales to dispatch conditions of surrender, which were
delivered to the aide-de-camp Louis-Antoine de Bougainville (Figure 54), who would later
gain fame for his travels and botanical achievements.

ATTAQUES DES FORTS DE CHOUAGUEN
en Amérique
pris par les français commandés par le marquis de Montcalm le 14.
Août 1756.
RENVOIS

A Le vieux Chouaguen B Fort George. C Fort Ontario D Camp retranché des anglais. E Traverse formée par les anglais depuis l'investissement avec des barriques de lard F Maisons & magasins incendies lors de l'évacuation. G Chantier de construction. Les français débarquèrent la nuit du 11 au 12 d'Août, pour abréger les feux de Chouaguen H Pente du coteau, qui en cachant les français aux yeux de l'ennemi facilitât les approches. I Parallele ouverte la nuit du 12 au 13 à travers les souches & les troncs d'arbres sur la crête du coteau. K Batterie de six pièces commencée dans la journée du 13. L Chemin, par où les anglais se sont retirés le 13 à 5 heures du soir, les français allaient ensuite occuper le fort Ontario. M Batterie de barbette de neuf canons faite pendant la nuit du 13 au 14 N Communication du fossé à cette batterie. O Rampe, qui conduit dans le fossé ou les français descendent jusqu'à la communication, sans être vus. P Batterie de mortiers & d'obus commencée le 14. Q Endroit, où les Sauvages sous les ordres de Mr. de Rigaud passèrent la rivière dans la matinée du 14. Les anglais capitulèrent le 14 à dix heures du matin, & se rendirent prisonniers de guerre.

C.P.S.C.M.

Figure 53.

The attack on Fort Oswego.
"Attaques des Forts de Chouaguen en Amérique pris par les français commandés par le marquis de Montcalm le 14 Août 1756. Dessine par Lieutenant Therbu. Grave par Contgen Frankfort." C. 1792. Engraved, 36 x 24 cm. Shows old Chouagues (Oswego), Fort George, Fort Ontario, the English entrenchment, the line formed by the English, and the route of the English retreat. It indicates that the English capitulated at 10 A.M. on August 14, 1756. (Personal Collection.)

Figure 54.

The French aide-de-camp.
Louis-Antoine de Bougainville. (Courtesy National Maritime Museum.)

Montcalm wrote to Brigadier General François Gaston de Lévis: "I am master of the three forts of Chouegen [Oswego] which I demolish[ed]: of 1,600 prisoners, five flags, one hundred guns, three military chests, victuals for two years, six armed sloops, two hundred bateaux and an astonishing booty made by our Canadians and Indians. All this cost us only thirty men killed and wounded." The loss of British troops during the actual siege was minimal, but following the formal surrender the Indians massacred some one hundred men. The British lake fleet, including the *Oswego*, also surrendered. The capture of Fort Oswego precluded the potential for an attack on Fort Niagara by the British and strengthened the French line of supply to Fort Duquesne.

Based on information provided by Bradstreet, Lieutenant General James Abercromby, who had preceded Lord Loudoun to America to serve as interim commander in chief, ordered Colonel Daniel Webb to reinforce Fort Oswego. Webb left Albany on August 8th and upon arriving at the portage between the Mohawk River and Wood Creek, learned that Oswego had capitulated.

Earlier that month, the French and their Indian allies attacked Fort Granville on the Juniata River in Pennsylvania and captured its inhabitants. On the Ohio frontier, about one thousand settlers were killed during Indian raids. Lieutenant Colonel John Armstrong retaliated with provincial troops by attacking and demolishing the Indian village of Kittanning on the banks of the Allegheny River forty-five miles upstream from Fort Duquesne. The governor of Pennsylvania made a treaty with the Delawares and established an alliance with the Catawbas that fall. The colony of Virginia built Fort Loudoun at Winchester.

Throughout the fall and winter of 1756, Captain Robert Rogers and his Rangers patrolled the woods and waters around Lakes George and Champlain, noting Montcalm's intention to attack Fort William Henry. In December, Montcalm moved his troops from Fort Carillon and Fort Frederick to Montreal and Quebec, leaving a small garrison at each fort. The English did not take advantage of this move but withdrew instead to winter quarters in New York (Figure 55), Boston, and Philadelphia.

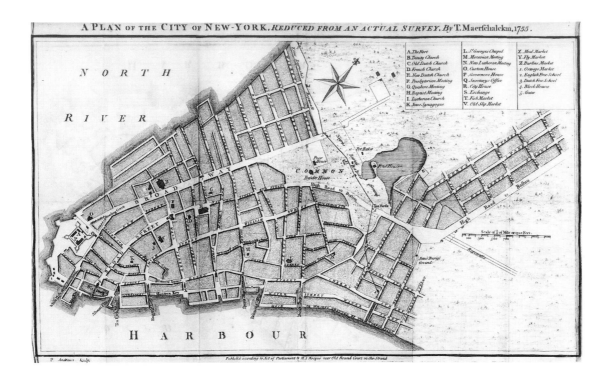

Figure 55.

British winter quarters.
"A Plan of the City of
New-York. Reduced from
an Actual Survey. By
T. Maerschalckm, 1755.
P. Andrews Sculp."
Engraved, 24 x 41 cm. In
*A Set of Plans and Forts in
America. Reduced from
Actual Surveys.* London:
[John Rocque], 1763.
(Personal Collection.)

6

1757

French Victories

Chronology

March 19	French under Rigaud deVaudreuil fail to take Fort William Henry.
June 20	British force leaves New York for Nova Scotia to try to capture Louisbourg, the gateway to the Saint Lawrence.
August	British aims for Louisbourg abandoned.

| August 8 | Montcalm takes Fort William Henry. |
| September 24 | Storm destroys much of British fleet off Nova Scotia. Year ends four-year period of defeat for British. |

Throughout the winter of 1756–1757, Rogers' Rangers, who had their headquarters on an island in the Hudson River near Fort Edward, harassed the French in the regions of Fort Carillon and Fort Frederick. At times they returned to the fort with prisoners or scalps.

The status of the ministry in Great Britain was as volatile as the war itself. On December 4, 1756, William Pitt, known as Pitt the Elder (Figure 56), was appointed secretary of state. Then he was dismissed on April 5, 1757, only to be reappointed on June 29th. His leadership in and appreciation for the importance of the war in North America was responsible for intensified British activity, increasing supplies and allocations of troops to the area.

The British felt that their prime strategy to establish control of Lakes George and Champlain in order to gain passage to Canada for a campaign there should be supplemented by a drive up the Saint Lawrence River to Quebec. This would require the initial seizure of Louisbourg (Figure 57), the French naval base and major port for the cod-fishing fleet from the Grand Banks and gateway to the Saint Lawrence River.

While the British were formulating these plans, Montcalm ordered a detachment of about twelve hundred men led by Captain Rigaud de Vaudreuil, the governor's brother, to attack Fort William Henry. The French arrived at the outskirts of the fort on March 19th. The English under the command of Major William Eyre repulsed four French attacks,

Figure 41.

Cartouche of Mitchell's first edition. "A Map of the British and French Dominions in North America...Published by the Author Febry 13th, 1755. Thos. Kitchin Sculp., Sold by And. Miller." (Personal Collection.)

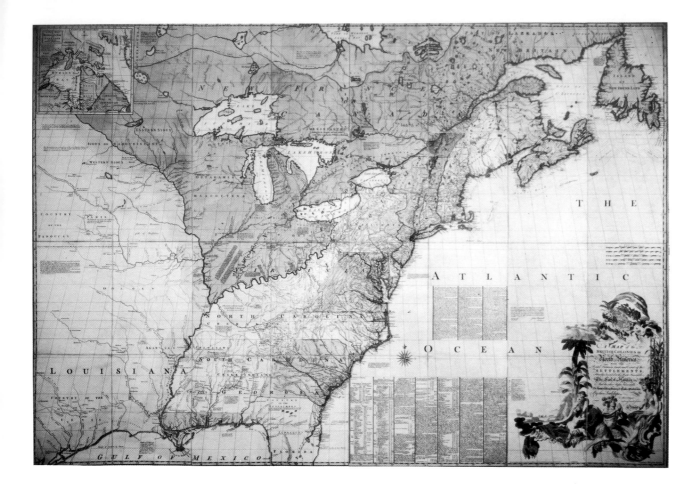

Figure 42.

Mitchell's 1755 map. "A Map of the British Colonies in North America with the Roads, Distances, Limits, and Extent of the Settlements, Humbly Inscribed to the Right Honourable The Earl of Halifax, and the other Right Honourable The Lords' Commissioners for Trade & Plantations, by their Lordship's Most Obliged and very Humble Servant John Mitchell." Engraved, contemporary color. 132 x 191 cm. Fourth edition. London, 1755. (Personal Collection.)

[Figure 43 is on plate 4.]

Plate 2   *The French and Indian War*

Figure 44.

The 1755 Huske map.
"A New and Accurate Map
of North America . . . [by
John] Huske. T. Kitchin
Sculpt. Sold by R. & J.
Dodsley." This map specifi
cally outlines all French
forts along the Mississippi,
in the Ohio Valley, and
along the Great Lakes, as
well as Forts Duquesne and
Frederick. London, 1755.
Engraved, contemporary
color. 41 x 50 cm.
(Personal Collection.)

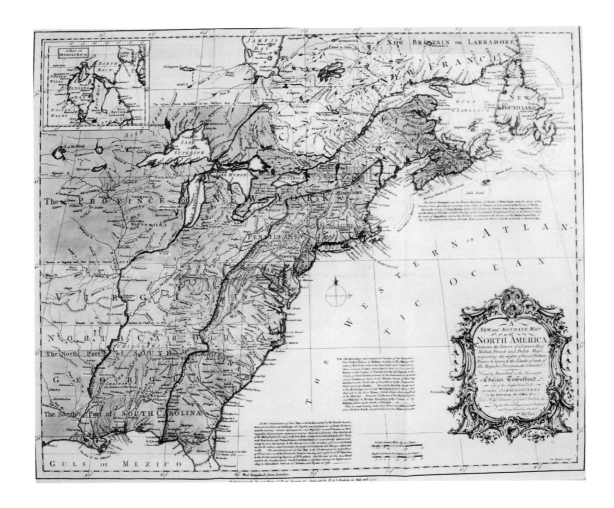

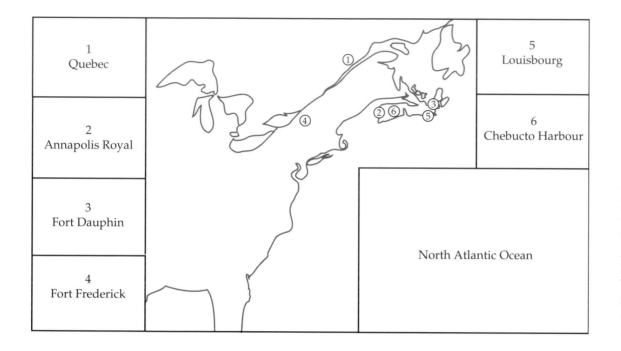

1 Quebec	5 Louisbourg
2 Annapolis Royal	6 Chebucto Harbour
3 Fort Dauphin	North Atlantic Ocean
4 Fort Frederick	

Plate 4 *The French and Indian War*

Figure 43.

The 1755 Herbert & Sayer map.
"A New and Accurate Map of the English Empire in North America: Representing their Rightful Claim as confirm'd by Charters, and the formal Surrender of their Indian Friends; Likewise the Encroachments of the French with the several Forts they have unjustly erected therein. By a Society of Anti-Gallicans." Published December 1755; sold by Wm. Herbert and Robt. Sayer, London. 45 x 71 cm. Contemporary color. (Personal Collection.)
Insets: "The Atlantic Ocean, A Plan of Chebucto Harbour (showing Halifax), A Plan of the Harbour and Town of Louisbourg on the Isle of Cape Breton, Fort Frederick built by the French at Crown or Scalp Point in the Year 1731, A Plan of Fort Dauphin on the Isle of Cape Breton, A Plan of the Harbor of Annapolis Royal, A Plan of the Town of Quebec." Chebucto Harbour is now called Saint Margaret Bay.

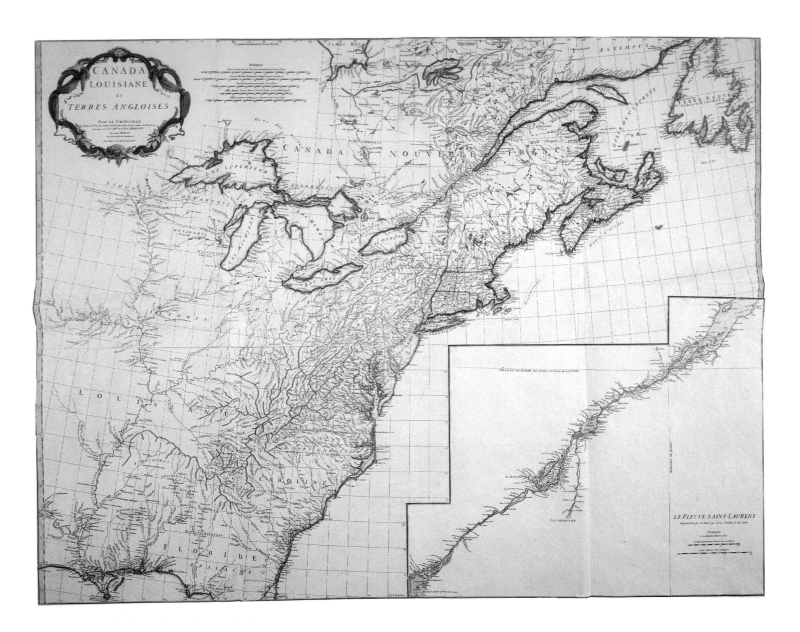

Figure 45.

The D'Anville map.
"Canada Louisiane et Terres Angloises par Sr. D'Anville." Inset of La Fleuve Saint-Laurent (Saint Lawrence River). This major map locates all French forts including Duquesne. Engraved, with contemporary color outline. 88 x 114 cm. Paris, November 1755. (Personal Collection.)

Figure 46.

The Bellin map.
"Partie Occidentale de la Nouvelle France ou Canada par Mr. Bellin Ingenieur de la Marine." This chart locates all French forts, including Duquesne, Le Boeuf, and one designated Abbe Piquct's compound. Engraved, with contemporary color outline. 49 x 63 cm. Paris, 1755. (Personal Collection.)

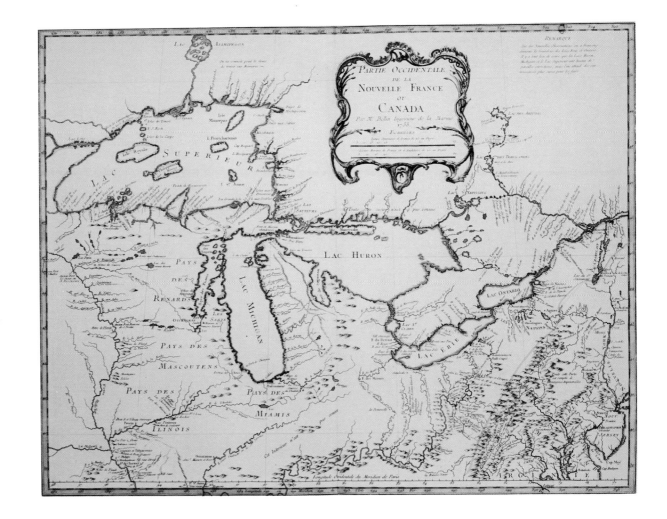

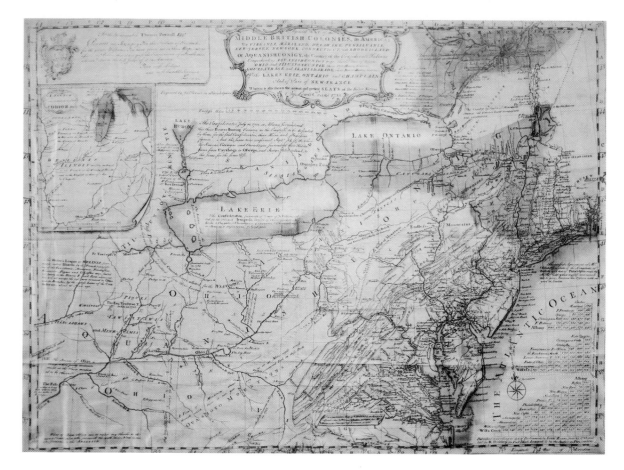

Figure 47.

The Evans map.
"A General Map of the Middle British Colonies, in America; viz Virginia, Mariland, Delaware, Pensilvania, New-Jersey, New-York, Connecticut, and Rhode Island;…and of part of New France; wherein is also shewn the Antient and Present Seats of the Indian Nations." Engraved by Jas. Turner in Philadelphia.

Published by Lewis Evans June 23, 1755, and sold by R. Dodsley in Pall-Mall, London, and the author in Philadelphia. 49 x 64 cm. (Personal Collection.)

This copy is printed on silk. Inset: "A Sketch of the Remaining Part of the Ohio R. &c." Includes three tables of distances: (1) Quebec to Montreal, F[ort] Frontenac, Oswego, Oxniagara Falls, F[ort] Detroit, and Albany. (2) F[ort] Duquesne to Oxniagara Falls, Sandusky, Tanixtanvier PictTown, G. Kanhanva Mouth, Lower Shawnee T., Wanviaxtas and Will's Cr. (3) Albany, Boston, NewPort, New Haven, Prince T., Philadelphia, Lancaster, New Castle, Annapolis, Alexandria, Williamsburg and Will's Creek. The map locates French forts including Duquesne, and the newly constructed British fort, Cumberland, in Maryland.

Plate 8　*The French and Indian War*

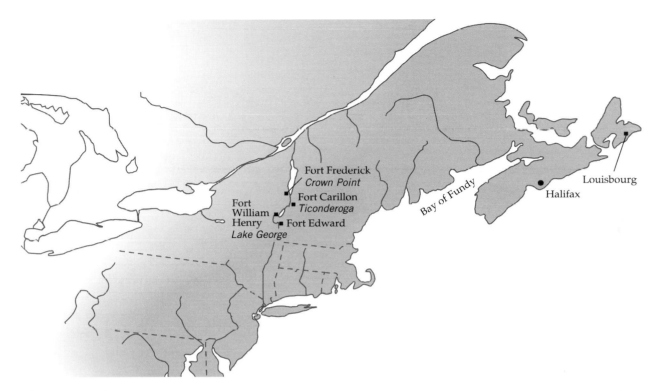

The war in 1757.

forcing the French to retire, their only accomplishment having been the destruction of several outlying storage huts and Rangers' quarters. Colonel Parker left the fort to attack the French advance guard at Ticonderoga but was surprised by a force that either killed or captured half his deployment of four hundred men.

Focusing on the main goal, the capture of Louisbourg, Commander in Chief Loudoun and his troops left New York for Halifax (Figure 58) on June 20th with a fleet under the command of Rear Admiral Sir Charles Hardy. Seventy vessels were used to transport four regiments, two battalions of Royal Americans, and five companies of Rangers. This force and the British fleet that had sailed from England under the command of Admiral Francis Holborne arrived at Halifax on June 30th. While the troops prepared with exercises in the area, Loudoun learned that the fort at Louisbourg was defended by three thousand troops supported by a large French fleet. By August the plan to attack Louisbourg was shelved. Loudoun and most of the troops left for New York, with some remaining to improve the garrisons at Fort Cumberland, near the Bay of Fundy, and Fort Edward, thirty-six miles from Halifax. The English fleet set sail to keep an eye on the French fleet, but on September 24th it was caught in a fierce gale that took many lives and cost a number of ships.

Figure 56.
William Pitt.
Secretary of State, 1756–1757. (Courtesy National Portrait Gallery, London.)

Figure 57.

Louisbourg.
"Plan of the City and
Fortress of Louisbourg,
with the Attacks."
Engraved, 12 x 17 cm. In
*A Set of Plans and Forts in
America. Reduced from
Actual Surveys.* London:
[John Rocque], 1763.
(Personal Collection.)

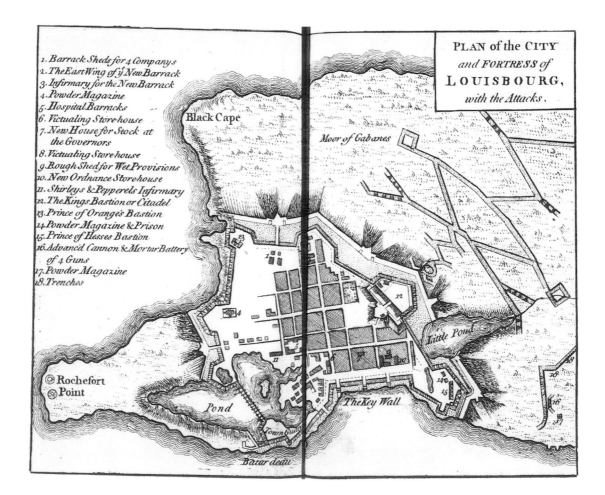

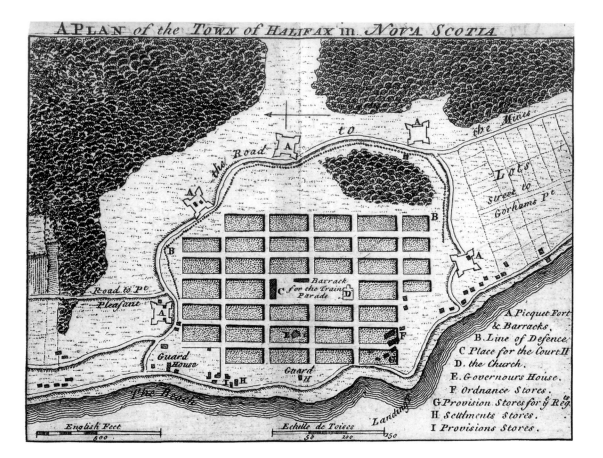

Figure 58.

Halifax.
"A Plan of the Town of Halifax in Nova Scotia. P. Andrews Sculp." Engraved, 12 x 17 cm. In *A Set of Plans and Forts in America. Reduced from Actual Surveys.* London: [John Rocque], 1763. (Personal Collection.)

At the time Lord Loudoun left on the Louisbourg mission, Colonel John Stanwix was dispatched with nineteen hundred colonials to protect the western frontier. The only forces left in New York were the four thousand men at Forts William Henry and Edward. Montcalm, seizing the opportunity, gathered a force of eight thousand French and Canadians and six thousand Indians at Ticonderoga. At the end of July, some went by boat, but the major force traveled overland under the command of François Gaston de Lévis. Despite having received intelligence of these maneuvers, Major General Daniel Webb, who had been left in command of Fort William Henry, elected to take no action. Then when Montcalm's forces appeared on the lake he panicked and fled for Fort Edward. Lieutenant Colonel George Munro was left in command of 2,372 men, of whom only eleven hundred were considered fit. The defenders heroically held out for four days under siege and battery attacks. Webb, who had under his immediate command fourteen hundred men at Fort Edward and at least another eighteen hundred in nearby camps, failed to provide relief. Fort William Henry capitulated on August 8th. When the gates of the fort were opened to the conquerors, the Indians wildly assaulted the inhabitants and killed many despite Montcalm's attempt to provide protection for those who surrendered. Those who survived either escaped to Fort Edward or were taken prisoner. The fort was demolished and the English boats on the lake destroyed or captured (Figure 59). The French elected not to proceed to Fort Edward, because they feared that English reinforcements would arrive, and most of the Indians fighting on the side of the French had left, sated by the carnage of their victory.

In the early fall, Rogers' Rangers captured prisoners during their reconnoiters around Ticonderoga and informed the command that only 350 French troops had been left in that fort, with only 150 in defense of Crown Point. However, the English elected not to attack these targets. The year ended a four-period dubbed by the historian Lawrence Henry Gipson as "the years of defeat" in the Great War for the Empire.

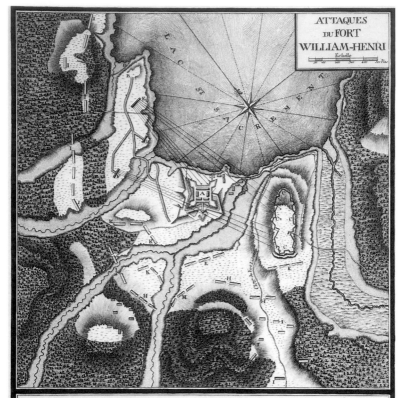

Figure 59.

Montcalm takes Fort William Henry. "Attaques du Fort William-Henri en Amérique par les troupes françaises aux ordres du Marquis de Montcalm Prise de ce fort le 7 Août 1757. Dessine par Lieutenant Therbu. Grave par Contgen." This rendering shows the entrenchment on the nights of August 4 and 5, the English entrenchment and the fort, the position of François Gaston de Lévis, and the position of the troops during the siege, as well as the troops of savages. Frankfort, C. 1792. Engraved, 36 x 24 cm. (Personal Collection.)

1758
The Tide
Begins to Turn

Chronology

May 28	British resume campaign against Louisbourg, Nova Scotia.
July 8	James Abercromby fails to take Fort Ticonderoga, despite having 16,000 men to 3,500 for the French.

July 26	Louisbourg taken; French fleet protecting Canada destroyed.
August 27	French surrender Fort Frontenac, on Lake Ontario.
October 21	British make peace with the Iroquois, Shawnee, and Delaware Indians.
November 26	French flee Fort Duquesne, destroying it; John Forbes renames it Fort Pitt. Jeffrey Amherst succeeds Abercromby as commander in chief of English forces in North America.

When the news of the failure of the Louisbourg mission reached England, Lord Loudoun was recalled and his second in command, Major General James Abercromby, was placed in charge. General Lord George Howe, whom Colonel James Wolfe regarded as "the best soldier in the British army," was Abercromby's deputy. Howe, impressed with the tactics of Rogers' Rangers, set out to incorporate them throughout his regular forces. Rogers was promoted to the rank of major and was dispatched to assess the French strength at Ticonderoga. He left Fort Edward on March 10th with 170 men and unexpectedly met 100 French and 600 Indians. During the ensuing battle approximately 100 English and 150 French and Indians were killed before Rogers and his men retreated.

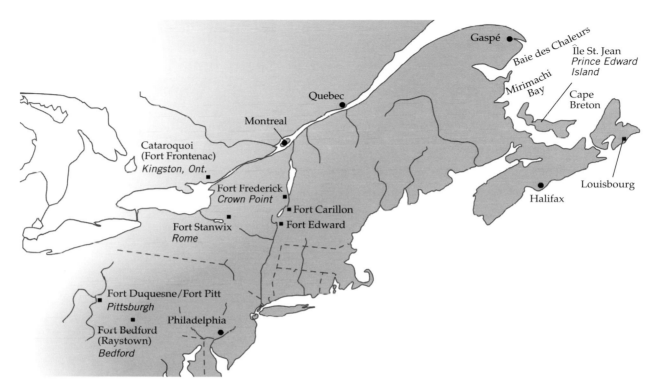

The war in 1758.

Louisbourg

Figure 60.

Sir Jeffrey Amherst. Portrait by Thomas Gainsborough. (Courtesy National Portrait Gallery, London.)

One of the major goals of the British campaign in 1758 was to capture Louisbourg. Secretary of State Willaim Pitt recalled General Jeffrey Amherst (Figure 60) from Germany and appointed him to command the land forces against Louisbourg; Admiral Edward Boscawen ("Old Dreadnought") was named to command the fleet in the attack.

Amherst sailed from England in March and arrived in Halifax on May 28th. His troops, made up of more than eleven thousand men, boarded Boscawen's ships and sailed for Cape Breton, which they reached on June 2nd. Bad weather delayed the attack until June 8th, when three divisions under the command of Brigadier General Wolfe, Brigadier General Edward Whitmore, and Brigadier General Charles Lawrence rowed ashore. At the time, there were five French battalions, consisting of three thousand regulars, stationed in Louisbourg (Figure 61). On June 12th, Wolfe's troops took possession of Lighthouse Point and gained control of that southeast side of the harbor. Foul weather interfered with landing more troops and bombarding the fort. The French answered with cannon fire directed at the British batteries. On June 22nd, British shells caused fires throughout the citadel, and the British batteries intensified their attack, with significant success. After forty-nine days of bombardment, the French capitulated, on July 26, 1758 (Figure 62). English losses included 21 officers and 146 troops, while the French had 350 killed and wounded. More than five thousand

Figure 61.

The attack on Louisbourg. "The Fleet commanded by the Honble. Adml. Boscawen, the Army by Major Genl. Amherst." Depicts the landing sites and the positions of the artillery. By T. Kitchin. Engraved, 30 x 70 cm. In *The History of the Late War in North-America*, by Thomas Mante. London: W. Strahan, and T. Cadell, 1772. (Personal Collection.)

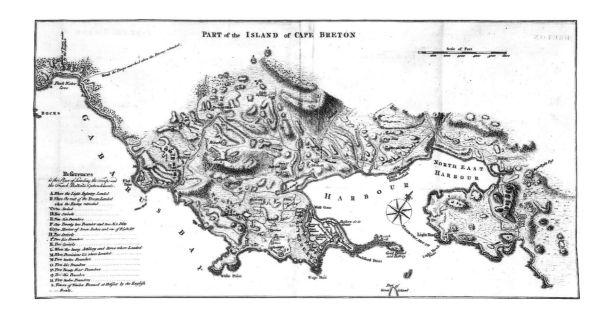

prisoners were taken. On August 7th Major Dalling was sent to Espagnollé (Spaniard's Bay) on Cape Breton to take possession and Lord Andrew Rollo accepted the surrender of the island of Saint John. Wolfe proceeded to the Saint Lawrence to destroy all French settlements along the shores of the bay and river. He dispersed and captured inhabitants of Mirimichi, Baie de Chaleur, and Gaspé. Col. Robert Monckton destroyed the French settlements on the Saint John River and took possession of Saint Anne.

During the whole engagement, the French fleet protecting Canada was essentially destroyed. At this time, General Amherst learned that the British attack on Ticonderoga had failed. He personally led troops to reinforce General Abercromby, arriving at Abercromby's camp on October 5th. Having left his troops there, he returned to Halifax.

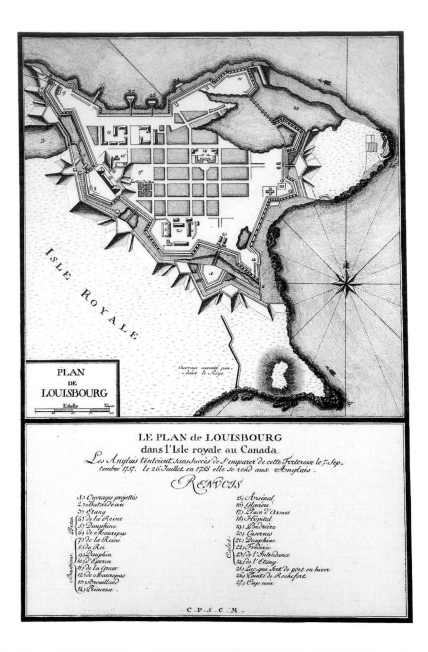

Figure 62.

The siege of Louisbourg.
"Le Plan de Louisbourg dans l'Isle royale au Canada. Dessine par T. Seibel, Bombardier. Grave par Contgen." The subtitle indicates that the English had tried without success to capture the fortress on September 7, 1757, and that the fortress surrendered to the English on July 25, 1758. The gates, bastions, and docks are depicted, as are the arsenal, glacière, place d'armes, and hospital. Engraved, 36 x 24 cm. Frankfort, c. 1792. (Personal Collection.)

Ticonderoga

The two other British goals of 1758 were to capture Ticonderoga and Fort Duquesne. The attack on Ticonderoga was under the command of Major General Abercromby (Figure 63), who led a force of more than six thousand regulars and nine thousand provincials. At the end of June, an encampment was established where Fort William Henry had formerly stood. On July 5th, the troops embarked, using more than one thousand small boats. The leading segment included the light infantry under Lieutenant Colonel Thomas Gage and Major Robert Rogers and his Rangers. The main body of the army was led by General Lord George Howe with seven regiments of regulars in the center. They were flanked by several provincial regiments, with the rear brought up by artillery flatboats and more provincials. They proceeded to the Narrows (see Figure 72), where they landed and began their march to Fort Carillon, where Montcalm had gathered about thirty-five hundred men. Ticonderoga was strategically positioned so that only one side could be attacked by land.

Rogers led the advance with two provincial regiments and Howe followed. In the woods, Howe encountered five hundred French troops led by Captain Langy, and engaged them in battle, taking 150 prisoners and killing the rest. Although the English lost fewer than forty men, that number included Howe. This loss of leadership led to marked confusion among the British troops, the majority of whom returned to their landing place, failing to take advantage of their gains.

Colonel John Bradstreet remained with about seven thousand men to occupy the French post and sawmills. Lieutenant Colonel Bradstreet requested permission to attack the fort before French reinforcements could arrive but Abercromby denied it, preferring to wait until the main body of his troops came up. This delay offered Montcalm the opportunity to bring in troops from nearby Fort Frederick and to construct entrenchments to impair a British advance. When Sir William Johnson arrived with four hundred Indians to join Abercromby, he was sent to command the heights known as Mount Defiance.

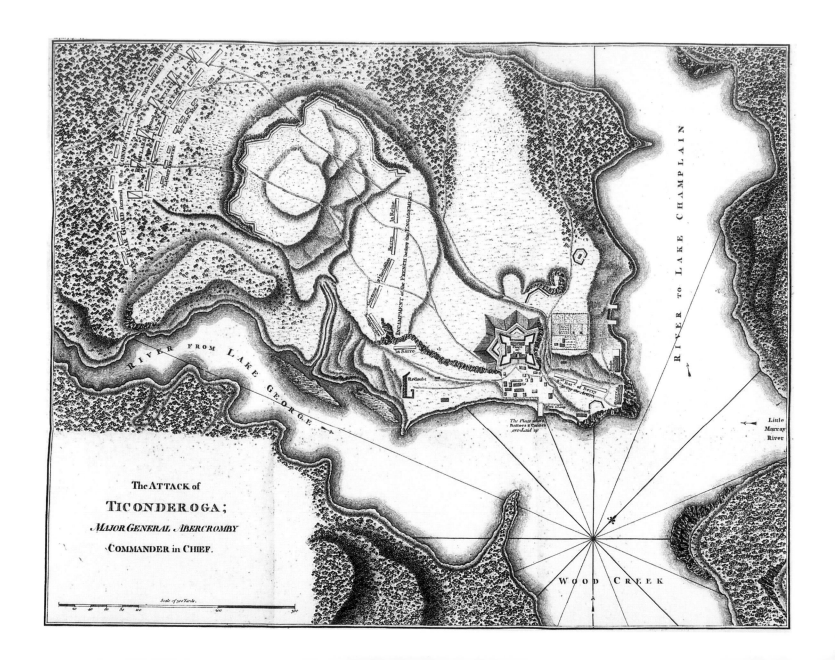

The ATTACK of

TICONDEROGA;

MAJOR GENERAL ABERCROMBY

COMMANDER in CHIEF.

RIVER FROM LAKE GEORGE

RIVER TO LAKE CHAMPLAIN

WOOD CREEK

Little Murray River

INCAMPMENT of the FRENCH before the ENGLISH arrived

la Sarre

la Reine

Redoubt

The Place where Battoes & Canoes are laid up

Scale of 300 Yards.

Figure 63.

Ticonderoga.
"The Attack of
Ticonderoga; Major
General Abercromby,
Commander in Chief."
Engraved, 37 x 48 cm.
In *The History of the Late
War in North America*, by
Thomas Mante. London:
W. Strahan, and T. Cadell,
1772. (Personal
Collection.)

Abercromby then decided to launch an attack without the aid of his artillery. On July 8th, the British attacked the fort's breastworks and tried to scale them but were beaten back by Montcalm, who had already prepared to retreat. The British troops then became confused, a confusion compounded when Abercromby turned his army around and returned to Albany. The British losses in comparison to those of the French were great. Of the English force, 1,944 were killed or wounded, whereas the French lost only 377 men. The French had won a victory against overwhelming odds as a consequence of a lack of leadership on the part of the British general (Figure 64). In July, French troops destroyed several convoys near Fort Edward. Major Rogers was sent to seek out the enemy and on August 8th was attacked by about five hundred French troops, which he defeated.

Lake Ontario

In an attempt to compensate for the defeat at Ticonderoga, Abercromby sent John Stanwix, at this point a brigadier general, to the Great Carrying Place on the Mohawk River to build a fort, which became Fort Stanwix (Figure 65). Abercromby also gave Bradstreet permission to lead three thousand men in an attack on Fort Cataraqui (Frontenac) on Lake Ontario, within present-day Kingston. On August 13th, the contingent took off for Oneida Lake, then went by way of the Onondaga River to Lake Ontario, where they embarked. On August 25th they landed near the fort. As they were preparing to attack, on August 27th, the French commandant, Captain Pierre Jacques Payan de Noyan, surrendered the garrison of about one hundred men. The loss of Fort Frontenac was critical to the French in that it contained a large store of artillery and provisions and served as the main supply source for Forts Niagara and Duquesne.

In addition, the entire French fleet on Lake Ontario was captured. The capitulation of Fort Frontenac greatly facilitated the British expedition against Fort Duquesne. In October, Montcalm withdrew his army from Lake Champlain to Montreal and Quebec and established winter quarters there, leaving only small garrisons at Forts Frederick and Carillon.

The Western Theater

In late July, following a series of delays, Brigadier General John Forbes, designated to command the campaign against Fort Duquesne, assembled more than six thousand troops in Philadelphia. Lieutenant Colonel Henry Bouquet was named second in command. Forbes planned a deliberately prolonged march that would last throughout the summer, hoping that the Indians around Fort Duquesne would become impatient and leave for their homes. The Moravian lay missionary Christian Frederick Post was dispatched to the Indians in the region of the fort and convinced them that they should part with the French.

George Armstrong's rough map of the country west of the Susquehanna shows (Figure 66) a new road through Pennsylvania instead of the old road coursing through Virginia that had been developed earlier by Braddock. When the army had marched as far as Raystown, ninety miles east of the fort, Lieutenant Colonel Bouquet and two thousand men were dispatched to take up a post at Loyalhanna Creek, leaving a main force of about five thousand men. Bouquet thought he could reduce Fort Duquesne without the help of the main force and accordingly sent Major James Grant with eight hundred Highlanders and several contingents of provincial troops to attack it. The French, led by Captain François de Lignery, met them with superior force and killed or captured three hundred British troops.

The entire British force, under the command of Brigadier General Forbes, arrived at the new Fort Bedford (Figure 67) at Raystown on September 23rd. On October 21st, after a council of nineteen days between the Indians and English at Easton, Pennsylvania, the Iroquois, Shawnees, and Delawares affirmed peace with the English. The missionary Christian Post returned to the region around Fort Duquesne. This time the Indians declared peace with the English and refused to aid in defending the fort.

The French panicked and dismantled and abandoned Fort Duquesne and retired down the Ohio River. On November 18th, Forbes led out twenty-five hundred men from the Loyalhanna Creek camp who on November 24th reached Turkey Hill, normally one day's

Figure 64.

Fort Carillon, Montcalm's stronghold. "Attaques des Retranchemens devant le Fort Carillon en Amérique. Dessine par Lieutenant Therbu. Grave par Contgen." This chart depicts a plan of the fort, the French retrenchments, and the positions of the French and English. The fort was later named Fort Ticonderoga by the English. Engraved, 36 x 24 cm. Frankfort, c. 1792. (Personal Collection.)

Figure 65.

Fort Stanwix. "Plan of Fort Stanwix, Built at Oneida Station, By Provincial Troops, in 1758." Engraved, 12 x 17 cm. In *A Set of Plans and Forts in America. Reduced from Actual Surveys.* London: [John Rocque], 1763. (Personal Collection.)

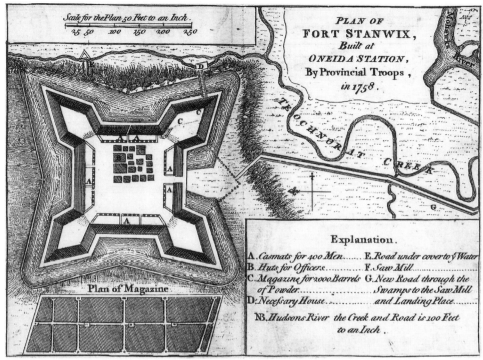

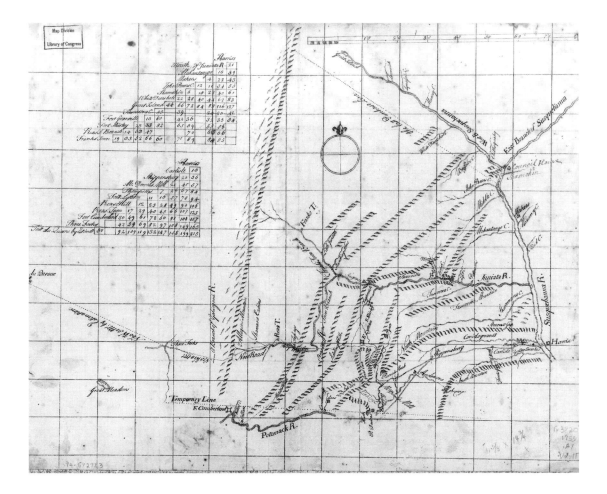

Figure 66.

Western Pennsylvania. "Mr. George Armstrong's rough draft of the country to the west of the Susquehanna." In the Pennsylvania Archives (vol. II, p. 483) a letter written by Colonel John Armstrong to Governor William Denny reads: "The General sent my brother George to Reas' Town [Raystown], with orders to take with him a hundred men, in order to find out and mark a road from Reas' Town as near to Fort Duquesne as he can possibly go, leaving General Braddock's road and the Yohiogaine entirely to the left." Manuscript, 30 x 37 cm. About 1758. (Courtesy Library of Congress.)

Figure 67.

Fort Bedford.
The new fort at Raystown,
Pa. Engraved, 12 x 17 cm.
In *A Set of Plans and Forts
in America. Reduced from
Actual Surveys.* London:
[John Rocque], 1763.
(Personal Collection.)

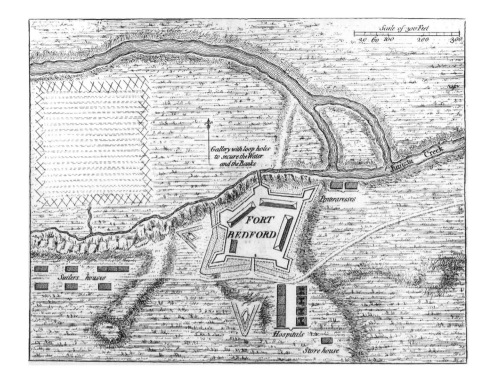

march from the fort. On November 25th the movement restarted with Forbes being so ill that he was transported on a litter. An advance guard was followed by Forbes, then by three parallel columns with Highlanders under Colonel Archibald Montgomery in the center, Royal Americans under Colonel Henry Bouquet on the right, and Provincials under Colonel George Washington on the left. When they arrived at the fort at dusk they found that the French were gone. The fortifications had been blown up, the storehouses and barracks burned. On November 26th, Forbes renamed the site Fort Pitt and rebuilding com-

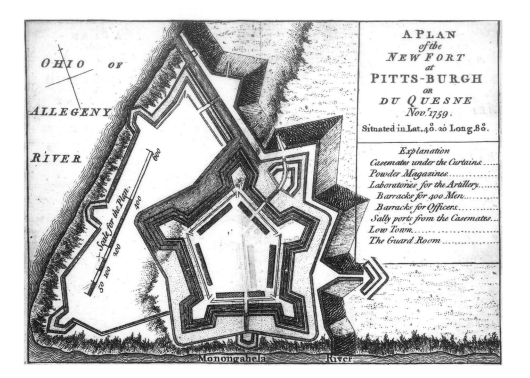

Figure 68.

Fort Pitt.
"A Plan of the New Fort at Pitts-burgh or DuQuesne, Nov. 1759. Situated Lat. 40°20' Long. 80°." Engraved, 12 x 17 cm. In *A Set of Plans and Forts in America. Reduced from Actual Surveys.* London: [John Rocque], 1763. (Personal Collection.)

menced (Figure 68). A garrison of two hundred Virginians was left and Forbes marched back to Philadelphia, where he died on March 11, 1759, and was buried at Christ Church. General Jeffrey Amherst succeeded Abercromby as commander in chief of the English troops in North America as the year drew to a close. The status of the war was depicted in a map by Louis Stanislaus d'Arcy Delarochette which indicates that the French surrendered Fort Duquesne, but it was published prior to the events that took place in 1759 (Figure 69. See plates 9 and 10).

8

1759

Victory on Three Fronts

Chronology

June 26	Fort Ticonderoga taken by Amherst.
July 25	Fort Niagara won by Amherst; Crown Point abandoned to British. Britain now in full control of the western frontier.

September 13	Battle of Quebec; Montcalm and Wolfe, the commanding generals, both succumb to battle-field wounds.
September 18	Britain takes control of Canada except for Montreal.
December 26	Treaty signed between South Carolina and the Cherokee Indians.

Although the most crucial battle of 1759 would take place in the summer and fall, far to the north, the initial engagement in the Western Hemisphere occurred in the Caribbean. The target of the British forces was Guadeloupe, the largest of the French Caribbean islands and the main harbor for the French privateers that threatened trade from the British sugar islands and North America. Bombardment by the English fleet began on January 22. The marines landed two days later, and articles of capitulation for the entire island were signed May 1 (Figure 70).

A three-pronged attack was planned for the North American continent. Major General Jeffrey Amherst, who replaced General James Abercromby as the commander in chief of all the British forces in North America, was to gain control of Ticonderoga and Crown Point, then proceed to join Major General James Wolfe on the banks of the Saint Lawrence River. Wolfe (Figure 71), in charge of another army and fleet, was to set siege to Quebec, the capital of Canada. The third arena for conquest included Fort Niagara, the lesser forts adjacent to Pittsburgh, and the line of communication between that region and Lake Erie.

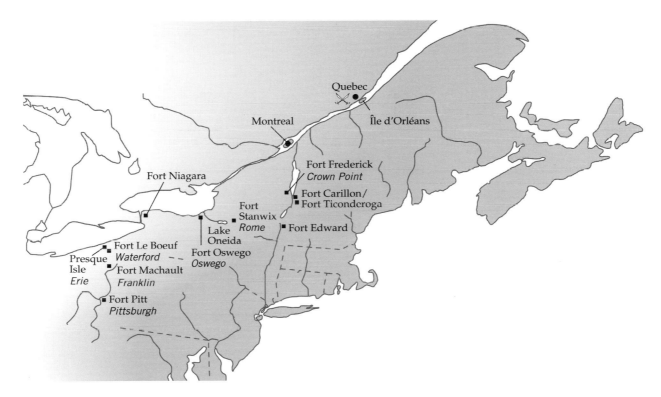

The following labels appear on the map:

Quebec

Montreal

Île d'Orléans

Fort Frederick
Crown Point

Fort Carillon/
Fort Ticonderoga

Fort Niagara

Fort
Stanwix
Rome

Fort Edward

Lake
Oneida

Fort Le Boeuf
Waterford

Fort Oswego
Oswego

Presque
Isle
Erie

Fort Machault
Franklin

Fort Pitt
Pittsburgh

The war in 1759.

Ticonderoga

Fort Ticonderoga (Figure 72) was the first to fall. Following Abercromby's failed attack in 1758, the French had reinforced Crown Point and strengthened their position on Lake Champlain. In March of 1759, Major Robert Rogers led a party of 350 men from Fort Edward on a reconnaissance mission to determine the French strength at Forts Ticonderoga and Crown Point.

On June 6th, Amherst arrived at Fort Edward with reinforcements and strengthened the defenses by erecting a series of blockhouses. Then, on June 21, Amherst left with six thousand men and established an encampment on the shores of Lake George. A month later the army embarked and proceeded to a place called the Saw Mills, where the troops camped. The commandant of the fort, Brigadier General François Bourlamaque, had been sent to Fort Carillon from Montreal with three thousand men under orders to avoid a major battle and, if attacked, to retreat to the Isle-aux-Noix. The French withdrew within the fort and emptied their cannons on the advancing British troops, but no damage was inflicted. After they destroyed the fortifications, the French troops abandoned Fort Ticonderoga on June 26th. Only fifteen British troops were lost in this engagement (Figure 73).

On August 1st, Amherst learned that Crown Point had been abandoned. He immediately stationed troops there and proceeded to strengthen and rebuild its fortifications (Figure 74). The French successfully retreated from Lake Champlain, despite efforts to thwart them. While at Crown Point, Amherst learned the fate of the Niagara and Quebec campaigns and therefore returned to New York.

Figure 70.

Guadeloupe.
"The Army Commanded by Major General Barrington. The Fleet by Commodore Moore." This map shows Fort Louis (now Fort George), and Fort Royal. Engraved, 48 x 57 cm. In *The History of the Late War in North-America, and the Islands of the West Indies* by Thomas Mante. London, W. Strahan, and T. Cadell, 1772. (Personal Collection.)

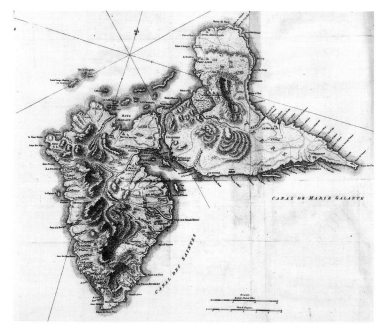

Figure 71.

Major General James Wolfe. The second in command in North America. (Courtesy National Portrait Gallery, London.)

Figure 72.

Ticonderoga (overview). "A Perspective View of Lake George" and "Plan of Ticonderoga." Hinton plan. Engraved, 26 x 16 cm. In *Universal Magazine* (November 1759): p. 293. (Courtesy David M. Stewart Museum, Montreal.)

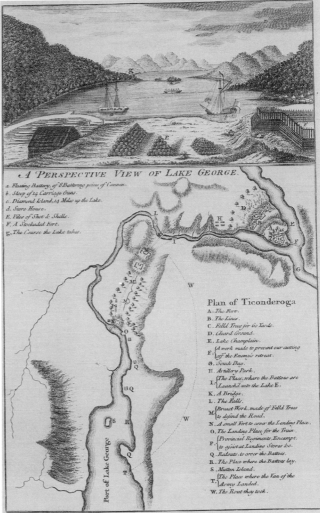

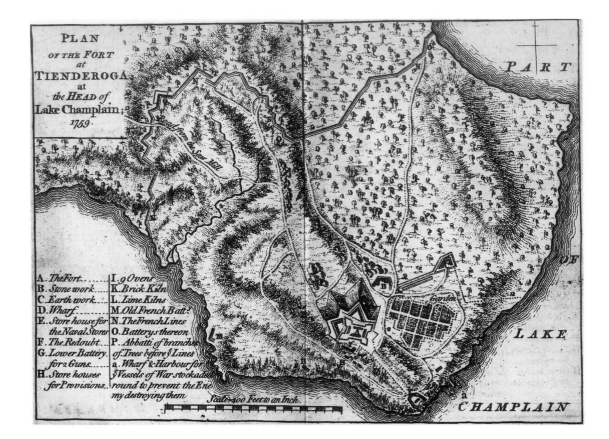

PLAN
OF THE FORT
at
TIENDEROGA,
at
the HEAD of
Lake Champlain;
1759.

A. The Fort.........
B. Stone work.....
C. Earth work.....
D. Wharf..........
E. Store house for
the Naval Stores
F. The Redoubt....
G. Lower Battery
for 2 Guns...
H. Store houses
for Provisions.

I. 9 Ovens
K. Brick Kiln
L. Lime Kilns
M. Old French Batt.
N. The French Lines
O. Batterys thereon
P. Abbatti of branches
of Trees before ý Lines
a. Wharf & Harbour for
ý Vessels of War stockaded
round to prevent the Ene=
my destroying them

Scale 400 Feet to an Inch.

PART

OF

LAKE

CHAMPLAIN

Figure 73.

Ticonderoga (close-up).
"Plan of the Fort at
Ticonderoga at the Head
of Lake Champlain, 1759."
This map shows the fort,
the redoubt, the old French
batteries and the French
lines. Engraved, 12 x 17
cm. In A *Set of Plans and
Forts in America. Reduced
from Actual Surveys.*
London: [John Rocque],
1763. (Personal
Collection.)

Figure 74A.

Amherst rebuilds Crown Point. "Plan of the New Fort and Redoubts at New Crown Point."

Figure 74B.

"Plan of the New Fort & Redoubts, at Crown Point." Both views: Engraved, 12 x 17 cm. In *A Set of Plans and Forts in America. Reduced from Actual Surveys.* London: [John Rocque], 1763. (Personal Collection.)

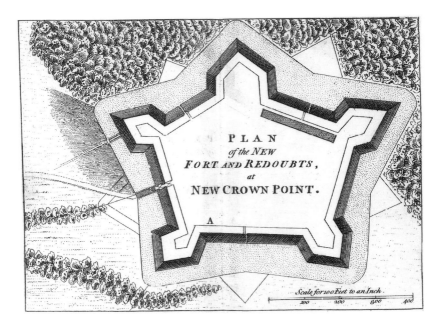

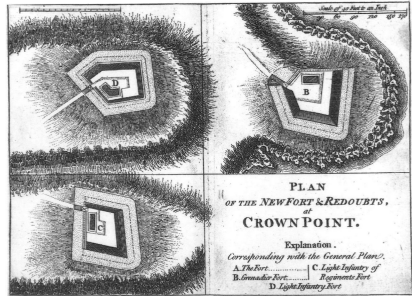

Fort Niagara also fell without a major battle. With Brigadier General John Prideaux in charge, twenty-two hundred troops consisting of two regiments plus three battalions and a detachment of artillery rendezvoused with a large body of Indians under the command of Sir William Johnson at Fort Stanwix. They then proceeded to Fort Oswego by way of Wood Creek, Lake Oneida, and the Onondaga River. A contingent of a

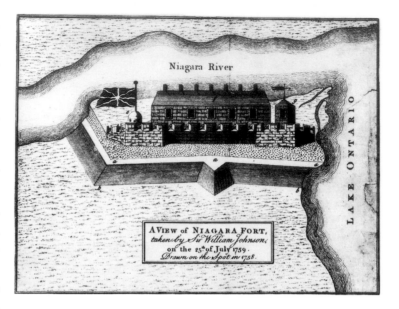

thousand men was left behind to refurbish Fort Oswego. The remainder left to attack Fort Niagara (Figure 75), defended by Captain François Pouchot with 515 troops and some Ottawas. Fort Niagara was a formidable fortification, triangular in shape and bounded on two sides by the waters of the Niagara River and Lake Ontario. The side facing land was well defended with batteries and bastions (Figure 76). Nearby, Captain Chabert Joncaire, a Seneca half-breed, commanded sixty troops at Little Niagara.

The English regulars and Johnson's Indians skirted the south shore of the lake and on July 4th arrived at Four Mile Creek, about that distance from Fort Niagara. When Pouchot became aware of the presence of the English he immediately sought help from the not too distant forts at Detroit, Presque Isle, and Le Boeuf and prepared the troops at Fort Niagara to withstand a siege. On July 19th, the day the bombardment was begun by the British,

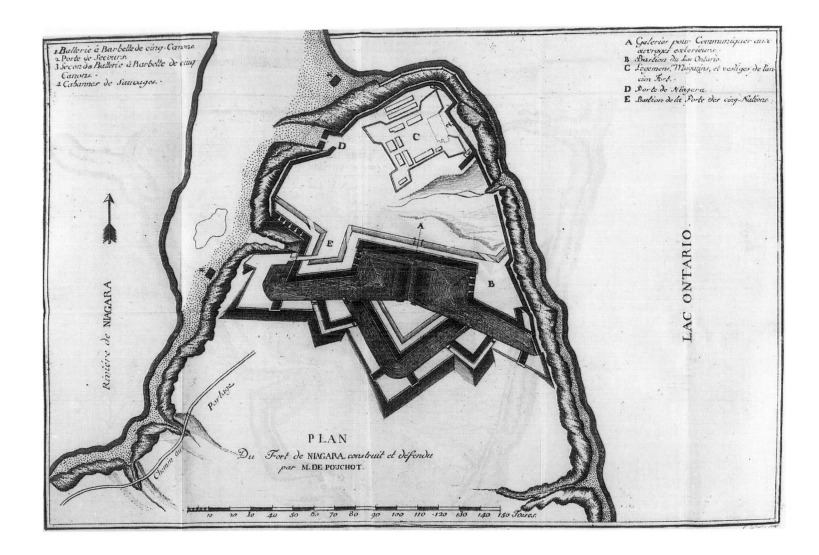

1. *Batterie à Barbette de cinq Canons.*
2. *Porte de Secours.*
3. *Seconde Batterie à Barbette de cinq Canons.*
4. *Cabannes de Sauvages.*

A *Galeries pour Communiquer aux ouvrages extérieurs.*
B *Bastion du Lac Ontario.*
C *Logemens, Magazins, et vestiges de l'ancien Fort.*
D *Porte de Niagara.*
E *Bastion de la Porte des cinq Nations.*

Rivière de NIAGARA

LAC ONTARIO

Portage

Chemin du

PLAN
Du Fort de NIAGARA, *construit et défendu
par* M. DE POUCHOT.

10 20 30 40 50 60 70 80 90 100 110 120 130 140 150 *Toises.*

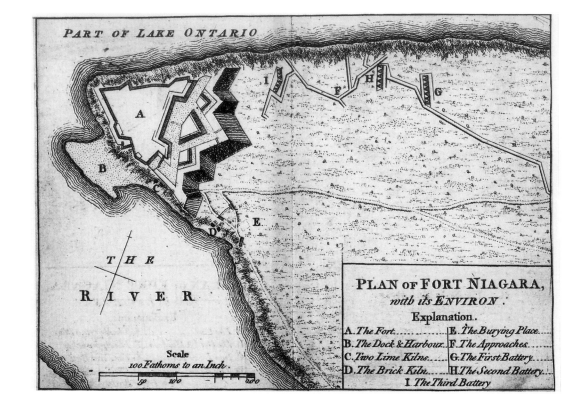

Figure 77.

Fort Niagara.
"Plan of Fort Niagara with its Environ." Engraved, 12 x 17 cm. In *A Set of Plans and Forts in America. Reduced from Actual Surveys.* London: [John Rocque], 1763. (Personal Collection.)

Prideaux was killed by an English shell that burst prematurely. Johnson, assuming command, immediately established an ambuscade at a place in the surrounding woods known as La Belle Famille, where the French reserves were ambushed. On July 25th, Pouchot, realizing that reinforcements would not arrive, surrendered Fort Niagara, thereby leaving the British forces in full control of the west (Figure 77). When news of the surrender of

Fort Niagara spread, the French burned Forts Machault, Presque Isle, and Le Boeuf and fell back to Detroit. At this point, no French fort remained between Detroit and Fort de Lévis, on the Saint Lawrence River.

During the attack on Fort Niagara, Colonel Frederick Haldimand had been left in command at Oswego. On July 15th, thirteen hundred Canadians and 150 Indians led by Captain St. Luc de la Corne attacked the fort but were repulsed by cannon fire and retreated to Fort Presentation and Fort de Lévis.

At about the same time, Brigadier Stanwix led troops to Fort Pitt and took possession of the forts at Venango, Le Boeuf, and Presque Isle, leaving Fort Pontchartrain at Detroit the only one in the Lake Erie area under French control.

Quebec

The most prolonged and memorable campaign of the French and Indian War took place at Quebec (Figures 78–82). The drama and consequences of the battle that culminated on the Heights and Plains of Abraham offset the minor scale and short duration of the battle itself to make the capture of Quebec one of the most significant military events to occur on North American soil.

The chronicle of this famous battle that lasted only some fifteen minutes actually began in mid-February 1759 when an expeditionary force under Admiral Sir Charles Holmes (Figure 83) sailed from Spithead, England, to rendezvous with Major General James Wolfe off Louisbourg. The ships arrived on April 21st and proceeded south to Halifax. Vice Admiral Phillip Durell had been dispatched to cruise the mouth of the Saint Lawrence River to intercept French ships carrying supplies. However, French ships arrived off the gulf earlier and sailed upriver to reach Quebec with reinforcements and information regarding the impending attack.

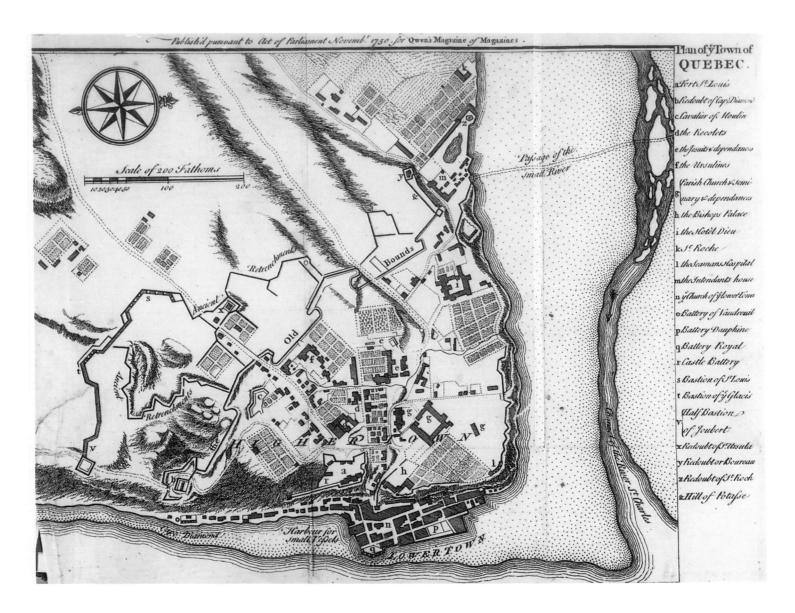

Figure 69A.

*Cartouche of
Delarochette's map.*
"A New Map of North
America wherein the British
Dominions in the Continent
of North America and on
the West Indies, are carefully
laid down from all the
Surveys hitherto made, and
the most accurate Accounts
and Maps lately Publish'd.
Also the French
Encroachments on the
English Provinces particu-
larly described." Map by
Louis Stanislaus d'Arcy
Delarochette, engraved by
T. Kitchin. Contemporary
color. London: John Bowles
and Son, c. 1758. (Personal
Collection.)

Figure 69B.

Delarochette's map.
"A New Map of North America. . . ." Map by Stanislaus d'Arcy Delarochette, engraved by T. Kitchin. Contemporary color. London: John Bowles and Son, c. 1758. (Personal Collection.)

Plate 10 *The French and Indian War*

Figure 95.

The Battle of Quebec.
"The Siege and Taking of Quebec, with a View of the Battle before the Town." By Henry Overton. From the *London Gazette* (October 17, 1759). Beneath the engraving are two letters to William Pitt: one from General Monckton dated "River St. Lawrence camp at Point Levi, Sept. 15th 1759" and the other from Vice Admiral Saunders dated September 20th, 1759. (Personal Collection.)

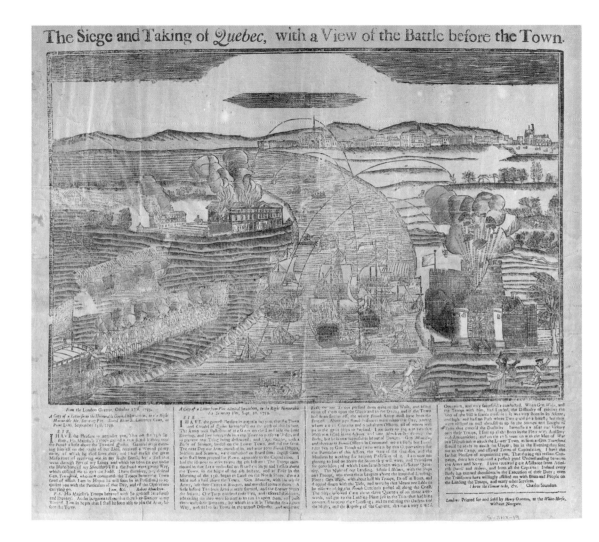

The Siege and Taking of *Quebec*, with a View of the Battle before the Town.

Plate 12　*The French and Indian War*

Figure 98.

The ruins of Quebec.
"A View of the Bishop's House with the Ruins as they appear in going down the Hill from the Upper to the Lower Town. Drawn on the Spot by Richd. Short, Engraved by J. Fougeron." Engraving, 33 x 52 cm. London: Richard Short and Thomas Jefferys, 1761. (Personal Collection.)

Figure 78.

Quebec: Detail.
"Plan of ye Town of Quebec." Identifies: Fort St. Louis, redoubt of Cape Diamond churches and locales of religious orders, the Hotel Dieu hospital, the Seamen's hospital, and various batteries and bastions. Engraved, 19 x 28 cm. *Owen's Magazine of Magazines.* London, November 1759. (Personal Collection.)

Figure 79.

Quebec: Landscape.
"A View of Quebec, North America." Engraved, 15 x 22 cm. (Personal Collection.)

Figure 80.

Quebec: Direct View.
"A view of the City of Quebec, the Capital of Canada. Taken partly from Point des Peres, and partly on board the *Vanguard* Man of War by Capt. Hervey Smith." Engraved, 16 x 27 cm. London: Carrington Bowles, (Personal Collection.)

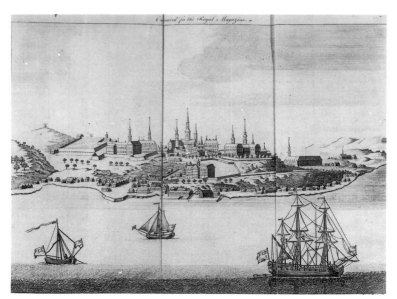

Figure 81.

Quebec: Perspectives. "A Perspective View of Quebec drawn on the spot." Engraved, 17 x 23 cm. *Royal Magazine.* London, 1759. (Personal Collection.)

Figure 82.

Quebec: Maritime View. "A View of Quebec from the Bason." Engraved, 15 x 24 cm. (Personal Collection.)

Figure 83.

*Rear Admiral
Sir Charles Holmes.*
Leader of the expeditionary
force from England.
(Courtesy National
Maritime Museum.)

The fleet carrying Wolfe's force of nine thousand men sailed up the Saint Lawrence, employing Lieutenant James Cook's extensive navigational chart of the river (Figure 84). On June 26th it anchored off the village of Saint Laurent, on the southeast side of the island of Orleans, a little below Quebec. At that time, Montcalm had in his command five battalions of regulars, colonials, and Indians—some sixteen thousand men—encamped along the shore of Beauport from the Saint Charles River to the Falls of Montmorency. Wolfe established a camp opposite Montmorency at a site on the Saint Lawrence's southern bank that had been abandoned by the French. On the night of June 29th, Brigadier General Monckton (Figure 85) occupied Cap Levi (Pointe Lévis), opposite Quebec, with little resistance.

Batteries were erected while Colonel Guy Carleton occupied the western part of the island. Attempts later to dislodge the British from these positions failed. These batteries effectively destroyed the lower town of Quebec and damaged the upper town.

On July 9, with the goal of threatening Montcalm's left flank Brigadier General George Townshend (Figure 86) established a camp east of the Montmorency gorge. While the camp was being prepared, Pontiac's Indians attacked, killing thirty-nine Englishmen, but were forced to retreat. Wolfe set up his headquarters and ordered Carleton to make a probing raid on July 21st at Pointe aux Trembles, thirty miles upstream. Few French prisoners were taken, and the raid was ineffective. On July 18th, several British ships sailed past Quebec. On the 26th, Admiral Holmes was sent to take command of the fleet off Sillery about three miles from Quebec. At that time a landing at L'Anse de Foulon, about two and a half miles from Quebec, where the attack was finally made, was suggested, but Wolfe planned to attack from the Montmorency encampment. Montcalm was forced to deploy three thousand troops under his aide-de-camp Louis-Antoine de Bougainville to the west of the city, to protect against attack from that direction.

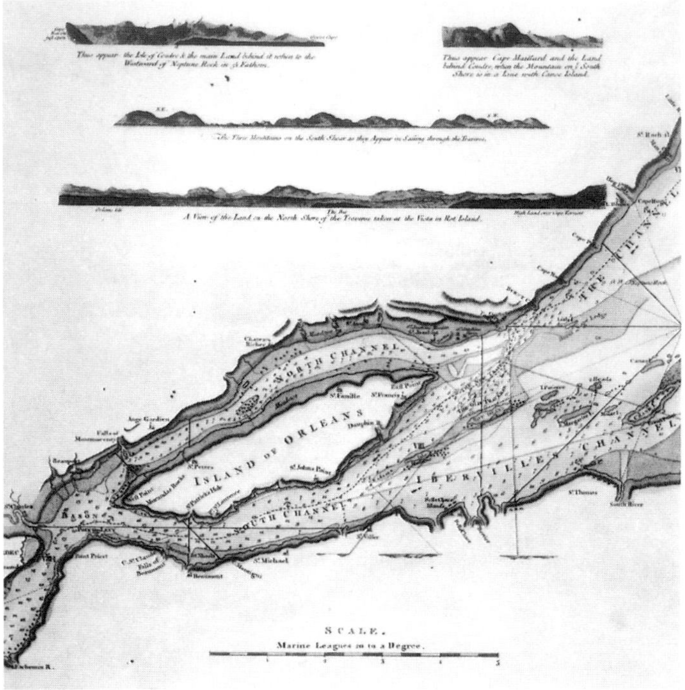

Figure 84.

Cook's Map of the St. Lawrence "A New Chart of the River St. Laurence from the Island of Anticosti to the Falls of Richelieu. James Cook. Engraved, 43 x 39 cm. London: Thomas Jefferys, 1760.

On July 31st, an attack on the left flank of Montcalm's forces began (Figure 87). Thirteen companies of grenadiers, accompanied by two hundred troops from the Royal Americans, Amhersts, and Highlanders, went ashore and rushed the enemy. They were supported by gunfire from the *Centurion* (Figure 88), which lay offshore. Four hundred and forty-three British soldiers were killed or wounded, a greater loss than that sustained during the final battle. The troops retreated.

On August 7th, Brigadier General John Murray (Figure 89) led troops to the ships above Montmorency, passing in the night in twenty-two flat-bottomed boats. Troops

attempted to land at the village of Trembles thirty miles above Quebec on August 9th but were repelled, with the loss of forty dead and one hundred wounded. On August 14th, Murray and his troops landed on the south shore of the Saint Lawrence opposite Pointe aux Trembles with a loss of twelve dead and twenty-three wounded.

The brigadiers met with Wolfe on August 29th and concluded that the strength of the enemy between Montmorency and the Saint Charles River precluded an attack there and that it was preferable to carry operations above the town. Accordingly, on September 3rd Wolfe evacuated the camp east of Montmorency and embarked on Admiral Holmes's fleet.

Figure 87.

Montcalm's left flank attacked. "The attack on Montmorency." Engraving by W. Elliot after Captain Henry Smith. The *Centurion* is directly offshore, Beauport behind the falls, Pointe Lévis in the background on the left. (Courtesy National Maritime Museum.)

On the night of the 4th, the first ships of Vice Admiral Sir Charles Saunders's fleet sailed above Quebec with stores and artillery (Figure 90). The following day, Murray led four battalions to a new encampment on the south shore of the Saint Lawrence. Monckton and Townshend followed, with three more battalions. By the 7th, thirty-six hundred men had embarked on twenty-two ships of Admiral Holmes's above the city.

L'Anse de Foulon, with its 180-foot precipitous ascent to the Plains of Abraham, was considered inaccessible. Thus its defense was left in the hands of one hundred men under the Duchambon de Vergor, who had surrendered Fort Beauséjour four years earlier. A storm raged throughout September 8th and 9th, forestalling a landing. When the weather finally cleared, Holmes's ships were sent back and forth between Cap Rouge and Quebec, to confuse and tire out Bougainville's following troops (Figure 91). Montcalm and his major force remained at Beauport. Then, on September 12th, Admiral Saunders began a

Figure 88.

*A model of
H.M.S.* Centurion.
(Courtesy National
Maritime Museum.)

Figure 89.

General Sir James Murray.
(Courtesy National Portrait
Gallery, London.)

bombardment of the main French force at Beauport in order to distract their attention.

In the early morning of September 13th, British troops landed at L'Anse de Foulon (Figure 92). The first landing was to be made by four hundred light infantry commanded by Colonel Howe and thirteen hundred regulars under brigadiers Monckton and Murray. The second landing was to consist of about nineteen hundred troops led by Brigadier Townshend. Half the French assigned to defend against an ascent had left to tend their harvest. Wolfe and Captain Delaune led the first group of twenty-four ashore. When they reached the top, Captain Donald McDonald answered the first sentry in French and indicated that the troops with him represented replacements. The encampment was thus captured without the loss of a man. Within three hours, forty-eight hundred British troops had disembarked.

On the Plains of Abraham the British formed up and began a march toward the walls of the city. A detachment was also sent to the west to capture the batteries at Sillery.

There was little cover on the Plains. Brigadier General Charles Lawrence's Royal Americans were stationed along the path from L'Anse de Foulon to the Plains, and Howe's light infantry remained behind the main battle line to ward off a potential advance by Bougainville along a road from Sainte Foy. Townshend's troops were lined up at right angles, to repel any attack by Canadians and Indians on the left flank. The main line consisted of about three thousand men, positioned two deep and one yard apart. The right wing, which was protected by the river, was commanded by Monckton. The center was led by Murray, while Wolfe directed the battle from a small hill on the right flank at the head of the Louisburg Grenadiers.

When Montcalm, responding to the sound of gunfire, reviewed the situation, he viewed for the first time the British troops assembled in line. At about six-thirty, a general alarm was sounded and the French troops began to assemble. Montcalm had some thirty-five hundred regulars for a battle line and fifteen hundred Canadians and Indians to be positioned in the bushes and along the flanks. The Canadians and Indians immediately began to snipe at the British troops from their cover.

Figure 90.

Admiral Sir George Saunders. By Sir Joshua Reynolds. (Courtesy National Maritime Museum.)

At eight o'clock a small artillery duel commenced. Then, opposite the British, the thirty-five hundred French troops under the direct command of Montcalm took their positions at nine in the morning. The French attacked the right flank and were repelled. At about nine-thirty Wolfe was shot in the wrist by a sniper and shortly thereafter took a bullet in the groin. Soon after giving the order for firing the major volley, he was shot in the chest and died on the field (Figure 93). Shortly after ten in the morning the French began their advance, in three columns. The British had loaded two balls into each of their muskets and when they were within thirty yards of the enemy they discharged their weapons in what was later described as "the most perfect volley ever fired on a battlefield." The

Figure 91.

Admiral Holmes's manuevers.
"A View of Cape Rouge or Carouge Nine Miles above the City of Quebec on the North Shore of the River St. Laurence." Capt. Hervey Smith (artist), Peter Mazell (engraver), and Thomas Jefferys (publisher). 61 x 84 cm. London, 1760. (Personal Collection.)

most telling fire came from Kennedy's 43rd and Lascelles's 47th regiments in the center. Then the British advanced and fired a second volley. The French were routed and chased to the Saint Charles River and into the town. Grapeshot mortally wounded Montcalm (Figure 94), who was carried into the house of a surgeon opposite the Ursuline Hospital, where he died that night. The pursuit of the French ended by noon. During the battle, fifty-seven British troops were killed and 607 wounded. Almost fifteen hundred French soldiers were killed, wounded, or captured. Wolfe's body was returned to England and laid to rest in the family vault in the Greenwich parish church. In Westminster Abbey a monument was erected honoring him. In a Quebec churchyard, a monument honoring Montcalm was erected.

The night of the battle, the French governor of Canada, Pierre Vaudreuil, decided that Quebec was lost and retreated to Jacques Cartier, leaving the Chevalier de Ramesay to make terms. On the morning of September 18, 1759, Admiral Charles Saunders and Brigadier General George Townshend signed the articles of capitulation. In the London Gazette of October 17, 1759, the first pictorial representation of the siege and taking of Quebec appeared (Figure 95. See plate 11). On December 1, 1759, a detailed

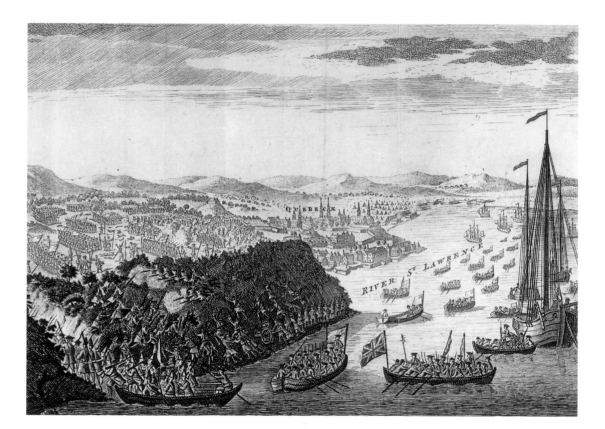

Figure 92.

The battle.
"The landing at L'Anse de Foulon and the battle on the Heights of Abraham." Engraving. London: Laurie and Whittle, 1797. (Courtesy National Maritime Museum, Greenwich.)

Figure 93.

"The Death of Wolfe." Engraved by William Woolet from a 1771 painting by Benjamin West. There were no Indians at the battle. (Courtesy Trustees of the British Museum.)

Figure 94.

"The Death of Montcalm." Engraved by Justus Chevillet from a painting attributed to François Louis Joseph Watteau. Montcalm did not die on the field. (Courtesy Trustees of the British Museum.)

Figure 95.

See plate 11.

Figure 96.

A contemporary map of the siege. "An Authentic Plan of the River St. Laurence from Sillery to the Fall of Montmorenci, with the Operations of the Siege of Quebec under the Command of Vice-Adml. Saunders & Majr. Genl. Wolfe down to the 5 Sepr. 1759." Drawn by a Captain in his Majesties Navy. Engraved, 19 x 24 cm. *Royal Magazine* (December 1759). (Personal Collection.)

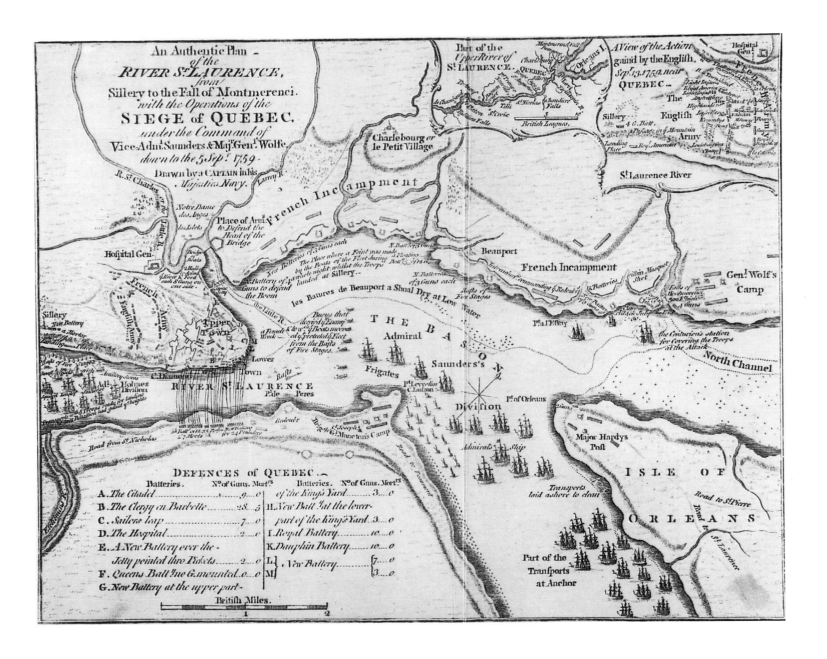

plan of the entire engagement appeared in the Royal Magazine (Figure 96). The first large-scale plan of the battle was published by Thomas Jefferys sometime in 1759 (Figure 97). Lt. Richard Short sketched scenes of destruction in and around the city of Quebec; a series of engravings based on his drawings was published in 1761 (Figure 98. See plate 12).

The British took possession of Quebec. Vaudreuil, Bougainville, and the remaining French troops withdrew to Montreal, the only place of consequence in Canada that remained under their control. Brigadier General Murray was left in command of a garrison of seven thousand men in Quebec. The French established winter quarters between Jacques Cartier and Trois Rivières. Toward the end of the year, the British directed their energies toward building redoubts outside the walls of Quebec. Outposts were manned at Sainte Foy and Lorette, respectively five and nine miles from the city.

The Cherokees

Far to the south, in South Carolina, the Cherokees continued to attack settlements on the frontier. After eight hundred armed provincials marched in Indian country as an act of intimidation, a treaty was signed on December 26th between Governor William Henry Lyttelton of South Carolina and Attakulla-kulla, also known as the Little Carpenter, the chief of the Cherokees.

The French and Indian War was part of a world-wide conflict, as shown on a contemporary German map depicting the sea battles and expeditions that took place in 1759 (Figure 99).

Figure 97.

The first large-scale plan. "A Correct Plan of the Environs of Quebec, and of the Battle fought on the 13th of September 1759." Engraved, 47 x 99 cm. London: Thomas Jefferys, 1759. (Courtesy David M. Stewart Museum, Montreal.)

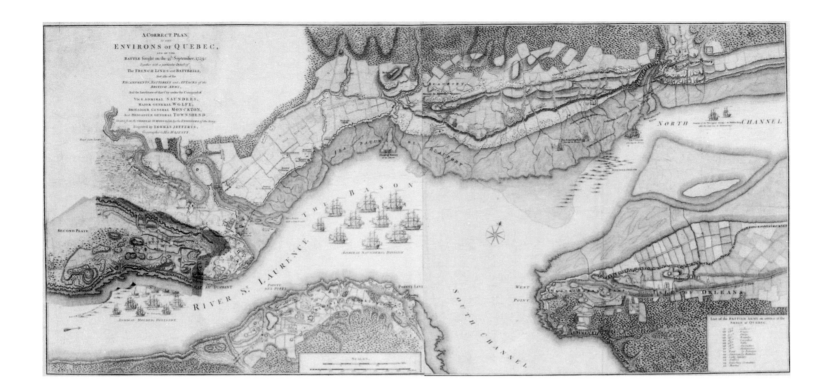

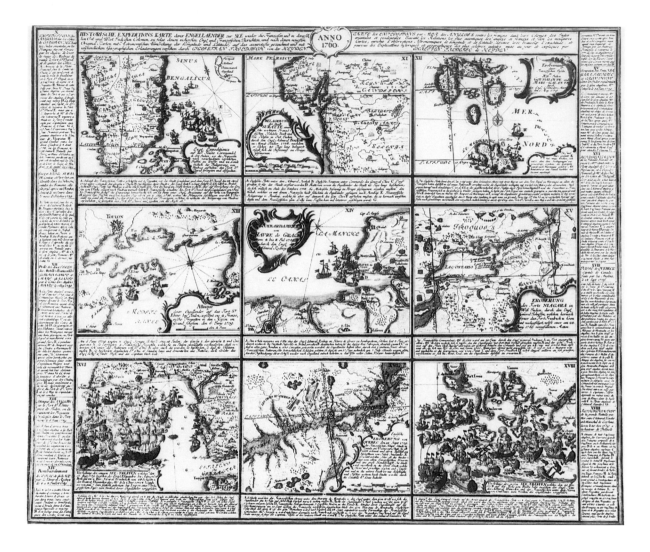

Figure 99.

A German map.
"Historische Expeditions Karte derer Engellaender zur See wieder die Franzosen" [Historical maps of English maritime expeditions against the French]. The map shows nine engagements that took place in 1759: (1) Off the southeast coast of India, April 28; (2) In the Gulf of Khambhat on the west coast of India, at the end of October; (3) Off Guadeloupe in the West Indies, January 16; (4) Off Saint-Elme near Toulon on the Mediterranean coast of France, June 6; (5) Near Le Havre in the English Channel, July 4–8; (6) Fort Niagara, Fort Frederick, and Crown Point, June 24; (7) In the Atlantic Ocean near the southern shore of Portugal, August 18; (8) Quebec, September 18; and (9) in the Bay of Biscay near Belle-Ile-en-Mer, France, November 20. Author unknown. Engraved, 56 x 67 cm.

Figure 99A.

The Ticonderoga Theater.
Detail of the German map
(Figure 99) showing the
engagements near Fort
Niagara, Fort Frederick,
and Crown Point.

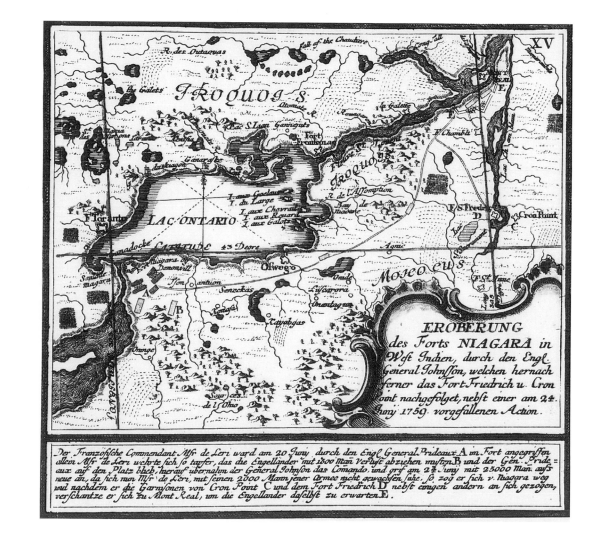

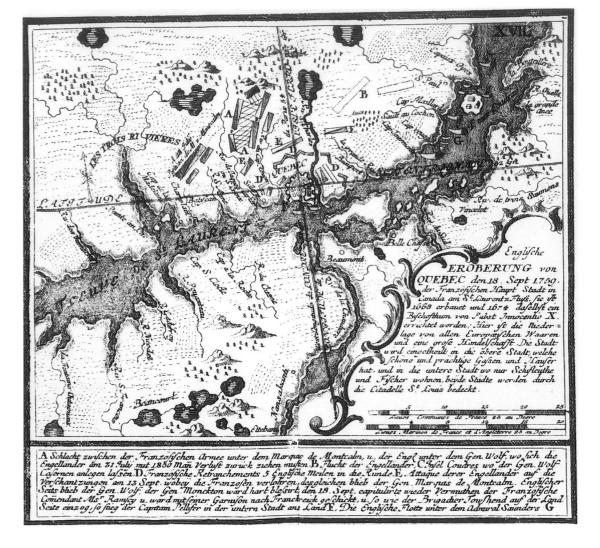

Figure 99B.

Quebec.
Detail of the German map
(Figure 99) showing the
engagements at Quebec.

9

1760

The Fate of Canada

Chronology

April 27	British attack French outside Quebec; British are routed back into city.
May 3	Amherst launches drive to take Montreal, the last French stronghold.
May 11–16	Siege of Quebec by French fails.

| September 8 | Amherst and Vaudreuil sign letters of capitulation completing the surrender of Canada. |
| About September 15 | British flag raised over Detroit signals effective end of French and Indian War. |

A lthough the British took possession of Quebec on September 18, 1759, the curtain did not come down on the drama in this arena until May 1760. The city that the British army conquered had been devastated. Brigadier General John Murray and the seven thousand troops garrisoned within its walls had few rations and rapidly became victim to illness, particularly scurvy. Efforts were directed at improving defenses against an anticipated attack by the French. The French indeed planned a spring offensive, under General François de Lévis. In February, French troops established a camp at Pointe Lévi, and Murray sent a contingent of light infantry to dislodge them. General de Lévis left Montreal with a force of about six thousand men on April 20th once the ice on the river had broken up. At the time, only three thousand British troops were fit for the defense of Quebec.

The French army proceeded to take possession of the post at Lorette and cut off the British troops at Sainte Foy and Cap Rouge. Word of these events got to Murray, who on April 27th marched out from the city. For the second time in six months, British troops assembled on the Plains of Abraham, but this time they were facing west, and this second battle was fought in reverse.

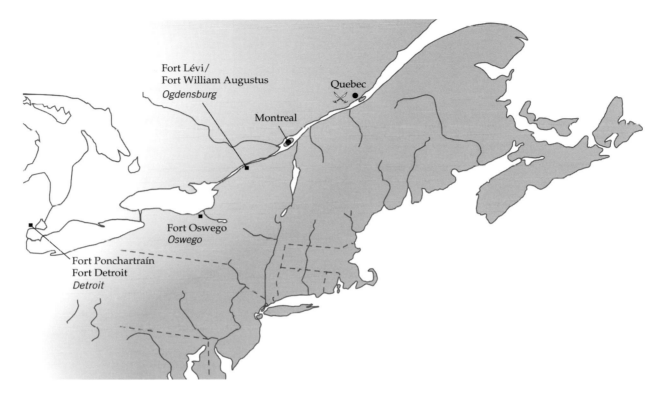

The war in 1760.

The British descended and proceeded toward Sainte Foy. They attacked the French in the woods around Sillery. However, in the face of the French superiority, the British forces became confused. Confusion led to total disorder and the British retreated to the walled city, having sustained a loss of some three hundred killed and seven hundred wounded. The French prepared to lay siege to Quebec.

The French attacked the ramparts but were repelled. Between May 11th and 16th, the batteries exchanged fire, until Commodore Swanton's squadron arrived with reinforcements and supplies on May 16th. The British troops now advanced across the Plains while their fleet attacked the French ships at Sillery. The French retreated to their quarters at Jacques Cartier.

The Cherokee Frontier

The early part of 1760 also witnessed hostile activities by the Cherokee Indians (Figure 100) against Carolinians, in flagrant violation of the treaty that was not yet two months old. They first attacked a settlement known as Long Canes, killing all the inhabitants. Then they assaulted Fort Prince George and enlisted the aid of hostages within the fort, but the troops repelled the attack and killed the hostages that had rebelled. General Jeffrey Amherst responded to a request by Governor William Henry Lyttelton for reinforcements by sending some twelve hundred troops under the command of Colonel Archibald Montgomery to Fort Ninety Six. In early June they attacked Indian settlements at Little Keowee, Estatoe, and Sugar Town, destroying all three. Throughout the month of June, Montgomery's men continued to seek out and destroy Indian settlements.

In August, after Montgomery's troops withdrew to Charlestown and sailed for New York, the Cherokees retaliated by blockading Fort Loudoun. The colonial troops capitulated and on their march from the fort were massacred.

Figure 100.

North Carolina Cherokee lands. "A Sketch of the Cherokee Country." By J. Lodge. Engraved, 28 x 38 cm. In *The History of the Late War in North-America*, by Thomas Mante. London: W. Strahan and T. Cadell, 1772. (Personal Collection.)

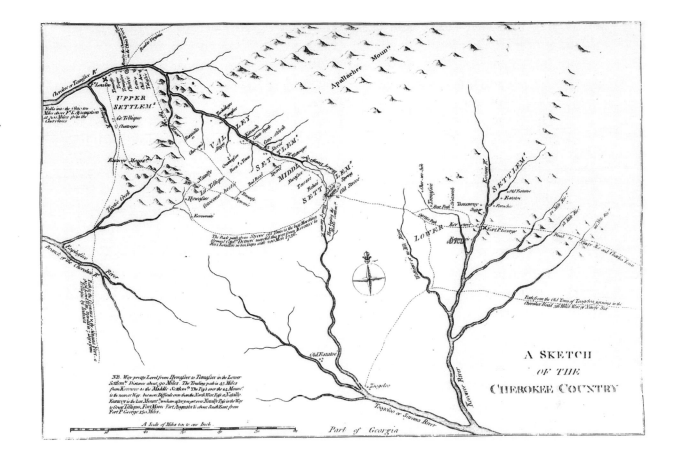

The Conquest of Canada

In regard to the French and Indian War, the year 1760 is remembered as the one in which the conquest of Canada was completed. To draw the attention of the French engaged in the siege of Quebec, on the 4th of June, Major Robert Rogers went down Lake Champlain and landed on the west shore, near Saint Johns. His British detachment of 250 men was attacked by 350 French and a battle ensued. Rogers's troops withdrew to the Isle La Motte. On the 15th of June he attacked and captured the small fort at Sainte Thérèse.

On May 3rd, General Jeffrey Amherst left New York with the conquest of Montreal (Figure 101) as his goal. On July 9th the British troops encamped at Oswego. When all the segments of the force had arrived and preparations had been completed, the army embarked, on August 5th, with more than ten thousand troops and seven hundred Indians, led by Sir William Johnson. The ships entered the Saint Lawrence River and on the 13th reached Point de Barril near La Gallette (Figure 102). From there, they proceeded down-river toward Montreal. On the 20th of August, following a minor exchange of cannon fire, Fort Levi on Isle Royal was completely surrounded by British troops (Figure 103). The assault began three days later. Under a protective barrage of fire from the fleet, the grenadiers prepared to land, but the ship carrying them ran aground. This chance event aborted a land battle, and the French commandant, the same Captain François Pouchot who had surrendered Fort Niagara, seeing that defense was futile, capitulated on August 25th (Figure 104). The fort was renamed Fort William Augustus.

On September 1st, Amherst and part of his army camped about ten miles east of Isle au Chats, where he was joined by Brigadier General Thomas Gage and another division the next day. The increased army proceeded past Lake Saint Francis and through the treacherous Cedar Falls, where several boats were destroyed, resulting in a loss of eighty-eight men. The troops then disembarked on September 6th at La Chine and marched the nine miles to the outskirts of the city of Montreal (Figure 105), into which the French army had retired.

Figure 101.

Montreal.
"A Perspective View of the Town and Fortifications of Montreal in Canada." B. Pomarede, Sculp. Engraved, 16 x 22 cm. London, 1760. (Courtesy David M. Stewart Museum, Montreal.)

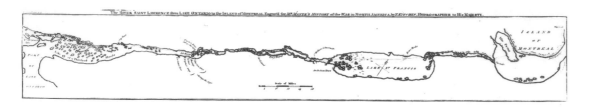

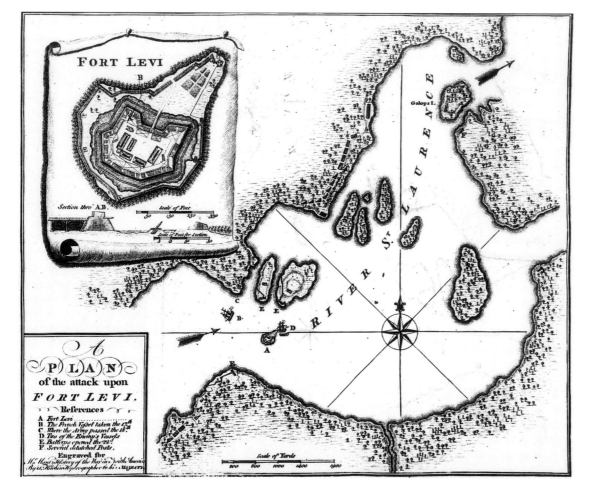

Figure 102.

The Saint Lawrence.
"The River Saint Lawrence from Lake Ontario to the Island of Montreal."
T. Kitchin. Engraved, 12 x 75 cm. In *The History of the Late War in North-America*, by Thomas Mante. London: W. Strahan and T. Cadell, 1772. (Personal Collection.)

Figure 103.

Isle Royal.
"A Plan of the attack upon Fort Levi." This map depicts the fort, a French vessel taken August 17th, the batteries opened the 22nd, and several detached posts. T. Kitchin. Engraved, 26 x 31 cm. In *The History of the Late War in North-America*, by Thomas Mante. London: W. Strahan and T. Cadell, 1772. (Personal Collection.)

Figure 104.

Battle plan for Isle Royal. "Plan Des attaques du Fort Levis sur le Fleux St. Laurens par l'Armeé Angloise Commandeé par le General Amherst Defendu par. Mr. de Pouchot, Capitaine du Regt de Bearn du 16 au 26 Aoust 1760." Engraved, 31 x 22 cm. In *Mémoires sur la Dernière Guerre de l'Amérique Septentrionale, entre la France et l'Angleterre.* By M. Pouchot. Yverdon, Switzerland: Tome Troisième, 1781. (Personal Collection.)

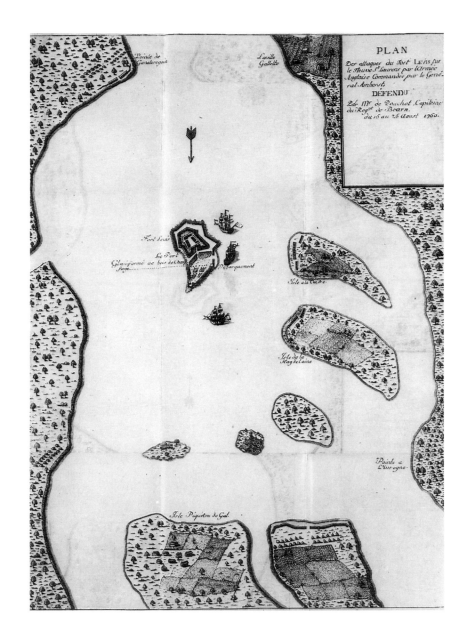

The capitulation of Montreal occurred without any opposition. In addition to Amherst's army, two British forces advanced toward Montreal from other directions. On June 14th, General James Murray and his troops had sailed from Quebec and proceeded west. Along the way, a contingent landed almost daily to terrorize the French inhabitants. The French could offer little resistance, and on September 7th, Murray's troops landed at Pointe aux Trembles without opposition. The following day they marched to the northeast side of the city.

The third army of attack traveled north on Lake Champlain under the command of Colonel William Haviland. On August 24th they captured the fort on the Isle aux Noix from which Bougainville had withdrawn. After taking position at the fort at Saint John, they established a camp south of Montreal on the Isle de Sainte Thérèse. Thus, on September 7th, the French at Montreal witnessed the advance of three armies coming from three directions and realized that any resistance would be futile. A series of letters between Vaudreuil and Amherst, conveyed by Bougainville, ensued over the course of a day in the absence of any shooting. On September 8, 1760, the two leaders signed the articles of capitulation completing the surrender of Canada.

One week later the final French fort in the Great Lakes region changed flags when Major Rogers raised the British flag at Fort Detroit. Britain had gained sole control of North America and for all intents the French and Indian War was over.

Figure 105.

Montreal.
"Plan of the Town and Fortifications of Montreal or Ville Marie in Canada." Engraved, 12 x 17 cm. In *A Set of Plans and Forts in America. Reduced from Actual Surveys.* London: [John Rocque], 1763. (Personal Collection.)

PLAN of the TOWN and FORTIFICATIONS of MONTREAL or VILLE MARIE in CANADA.

A. A Dry Ditch about 8 Feet deep
B.
C.
D. The Fort only a Cavalier without a Parapet
E. Recolects Convent Gardens
F. The Seminary
G. The Parish Church
H. The Nunnery Hospital
I. The Powder Magazine
K. Sisters of the Congregation and Garden
L. The Jesuites Church and Convent
M. A Small Chapel Burnt down
N. The Arsenal and Yard for Canoos & Batteaux

RIVER St LAURENCE

English Yards.

10

1761–1764

The Curtain Comes Down—Slowly

Chronology

1761	Peace with Cherokees.
September 18, 1762	French attempt to retake Newfoundland fails, ending war between the English and French in North America.

February 10, 1763	Treaty of Paris gives all of France's possessions east of the Mississippi (except New Orleans) to England.
April 3, 1763	Treaty with Senecas.
August 12, 1763	Delawares, Hurons, and Five Nations sue for peace.
September 1763	Forts Pitt, Detroit, and Niagara strengthened against Indians.
September 7, 1764	Treaty with Ottawas and Chippewas.
November 28, 1764	Hostage repatriation between Indians and British completed.

The state of events up to that time was depicted in a large map entitled "A General Map of North America; In which is Express'd The several New Roads, Forts, Engagements, etc., taken from Actual Surveys and Observations Made in the Army employ'd there, From the Year 1754 to 1761" (Figure 106). The year 1761 was distinguished by the absence of fighting and peace with the the Cherokees leading to a sense of security in the frontier settlements. In 1762 Lieutenant Henry Timberlake traveled throughout the Cherokees' land and three years later drew a map (Figure 107) that focused on the Indian villages and the number of men they could muster for battle. The year 1762 provided evidence of the worldwide nature of the conflict in which the French and Indian War was a major issue. The British now turned their attention to the Caribbean Sea.

Figure 106.

North America in 1761. "A General Map of North America; In which is Express'd The several New Roads, Forts, Engagements, etc. … taken from Actual Surveys and Observations made in the Army employ'd there, From the Year 1754 to 1761. Drawn by the late John Rocque, topographer to His Majesty." Engraved, 88 x 91 cm. The various engagements are marked by crossed swords placed at Forts Duquesne, Niagara, Edward, William Henry, Quebec, and Louisbourg. London: M. A. Rocque, c. 1762. (Personal Collection.)

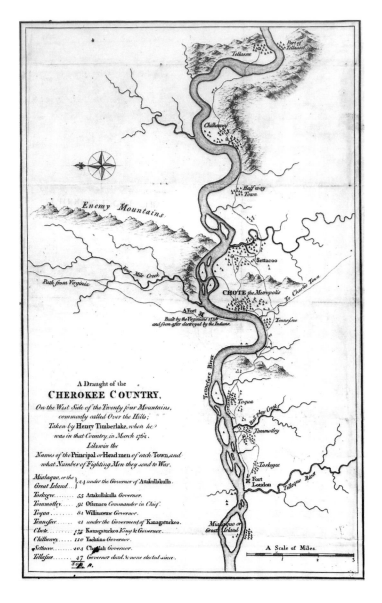

Figure 107.

The 1762 Timberlake map. "A Draught of the Cherokee Country, On the West Side of the Twenty four Mountains, commonly called Over the Hills; Taken by Henry Timberlake when he was in that Country in March 1762." Engraved, 40 x 24 cm. This map names the head men of each Indian town and the number of fighting men they could send to war. It shows a fort built by the Virginians and destroyed by the Indians in 1756. This is the first printed map of Tennessee by someone who had been there. Henry Timberlake, *Memoirs.* London: c. 1765. (Personal Collection.)

Figure 108.

Martinique.
"A View of the Coast of Martinico taken by desire of Rear Adml. Rodney before the Attack in Jany. 1762." T. Kitchin. Engraved, 29 x 44 cm. This map depicts where troops under General Hopson landed in a failed attempt to capture the island in 1759. In *The History of the Late War in North-America*, by Thomas Mante. London: W. Strahan and T. Cadell, 1772. (Personal Collection.)

On February 13, 1762, the island of Martinique capitulated to a British naval and marine force (Figure 108). Pigeon Island surrendered the same day, and two weeks later the island of Saint Lucia followed suit. Early in the year England declared war against Spain and immediately set its sights on Havana with its formidable fortress. Following forty-four days of battle focused on that fortress, Havana capitulated, on August 12th (Figure 109).

France, seeking to recoup some of its losses, planned to recapture Newfoundland. On June 24th, a squadron of four ships carried fifteen hundred troops to the shore of the Bay

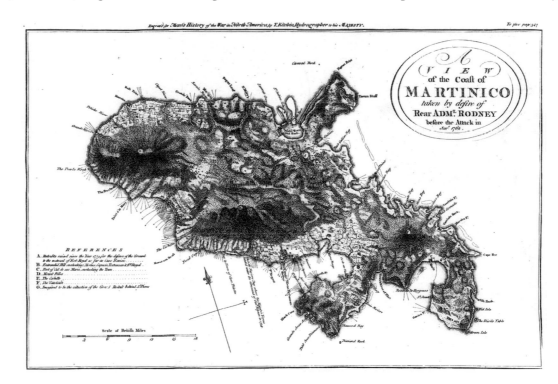

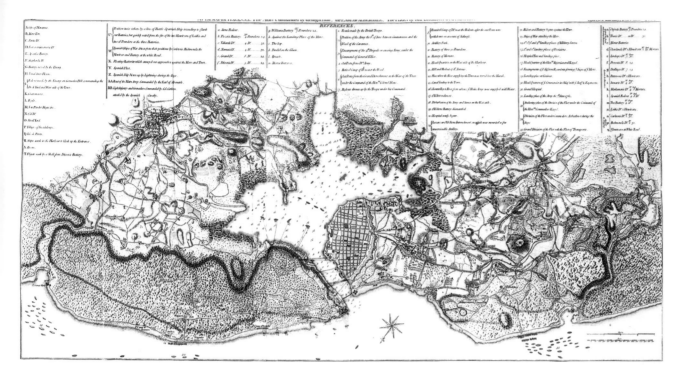

of Bulls. After landing without opposition, three days later the French captured the garrison at Saint Johns. General Jeffrey Amherst immediately reacted to news of the event by sending his brother, Lieutenant Colonel William Amherst, to join Vice Admiral Lord Colville, who had already left Halifax, to recapture the post and squelch the French plan. The British troops landed on September 14th without opposition and marched to take possession of a pass at Kitty Vitty (Figure 110). There the enemy was engaged and forced to retreat. On September 17th batteries were established outside the Saint Johns garrison

Figure 110.

Newfoundland.
"Plan of the Retaking Newfoundland, the Squadron commanded by Lord Colville, the Troops by Lieut. Col. Amherst." T. Kitchin. Engraved, 21 x 31cm. This rendering details the English position on September 13th and 15th and shows the main batteries. In *The History of the Late War in North-America*, by Thomas Mante. London: W. Strahan and T. Cadell, 1772. (Personal Collection.)

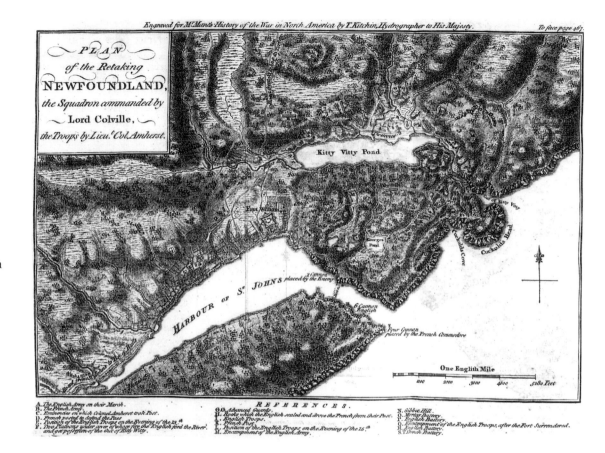

and bombardment began. The next day the French surrendered, leaving Newfoundland in British hands and ending the war between the English and French in North America.

The Treaty of Paris was signed at Versailles on February 10, 1763. By it France surrendered all her possessions east of the Mississippi River, with the exception of New Orleans, to Great Britain. France then deeded New Orleans and the large expanse of land west of the Mississippi to Spain. This compensated Spain for surrendering Florida to the British; the British in turn allowed Spain to retain control of Havana. France retained the islands of Saint Pierre and Miquelon in the Gulf of Saint Lawrence as bases for fishermen and regained the Caribbean islands of Martinique, Guadeloupe, and Saint Lucia.

The Indians alone remained hostile. In April 1763, encouraged by Canadian frontiersmen of mixed parentage, several tribes banded together under the leadership of Pontiac (Figure 111) in an effort to regain control of the Ohio Valley. The Shawnees, Delawares, and other tribes harassed frontiersmen and their families during the harvest, scalping and killing many. Western parts of Pennsylvania, Maryland, and Virginia were under a constant threat. Almost simultaneously, the

Figure 111.

Pontiac, chief of the Ottawas. (Courtesy of the Museum of the American Indian, Heye Foundation, New York.)

Indians attacked and took possession of forts at Le Boeuf, Venango, Presque Isle, Sandusky, La Baie, and outposts on the Saint Joseph River, Miami River, the Ouabache (Wabash) River and at Michilimackinac. All the garrisons at these forts were weak and were dependent on the Indians for their supplies. Fort Niagara was not attacked, but Forts Pitt and the Detroit were blockaded and exposed to Indian attack.

Sir Jeffrey Amherst, the British commander in chief, dispatched troops led by Captain James Dalyell, his aide-de-camp, to reinforce Niagara and Detroit. After a contingent took off for Niagara, the remainder continued on to Detroit, where they arrived on July 30th. Dalyell left the fort there with 250 men on July 31st to engage the Indians in the region. The British were confronted by a superior force of Indians causing them to retreat, but not before Captain Dalyell and nineteen soldiers were killed.

Major Henry Gladwin, who commanded the post at Detroit (Figure 112) continued to trade blows with the Indians. The schooner *Huron*, which was bringing supplies to the fort, anchored at the mouth of the river. Indians attacked the vessel, but failed to capture it and suffered heavy casualties. The Indians led by Pontiac lost their enthusiasm for battle because of the lack of significant victories and the deaths of several chiefs. Pontiac capitulated on October 31, 1763 (Figure 113).

Colonel Henry Bouquet was dispatched with troops to relieve Fort Pitt. Fort Ligonier, which contained provisions for the relief of Fort Pitt, was also in danger. Two companies of light infantry sent to reinforce Fort Ligonier were joined by troops from Fort Bedford, thus negating any plan for an Indian attack.

Bouquet assembled his troops at Carlisle, Pennsylvania, and marched to Fort Bedford, arriving on July 25th. When the Indians learned of his presence, they raised their siege of Fort Pitt and concentrated their forces for an attack on the British troops. Bouquet moved his troops to Fort Ligonier on July 28th. After leaving stores there, he proceeded toward Fort Pitt. They stopped at Bushy Run, a creek to the east of Fort Pitt, to refresh the men and horses and on the night of August 4th set out for their destination.

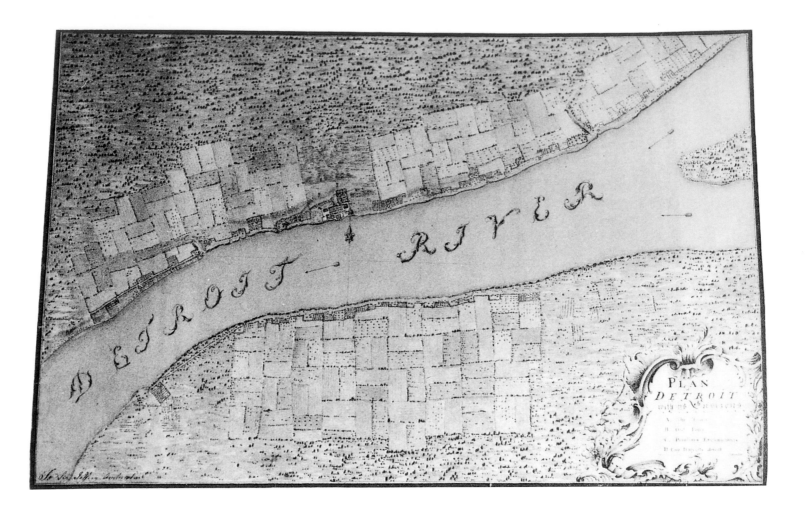

Figure 112.

Detroit River.
Manuscript map by Lt. John Montresor. (Courtesy William Clements Library, University of Michigan.)

Figure 113.

Pontiac's note of capitulation.
(Courtesy William Clements Library, University of Michigan.)

Mon Frere

La Parole que mon Pere a envoyée pour faire la Paix je l'accepte tous mes jeunes Gens ont enterrés leurs Cassetetes je pense que tu oublieras les mauvaises choses qui sont passées il y a quelque tems; de memes j'oublirai ce que tu peut m'avoir fait pour ne penser que de bonne, moi, les Saulteurs, les Hurons, nous devons t'aller parler quand tu nous demanderas, fais nous la Reponse, je t'envoye le Conseil afin que tu le voye, si tu es bien comme moi tu me feras reponse. Je te souhait le bon Jour.

A Monsieur
Monsr. Gladwin Major
Commandt. au Detroit.

signé Pondiak

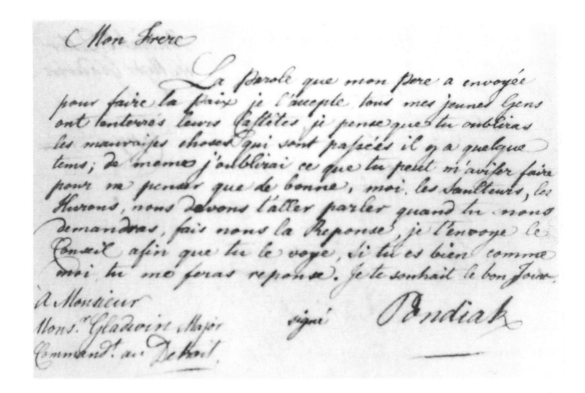

The following day the advance guard was attacked by Indians from one side of the road. More troops were sent to the area of attack and drove the Indians back. The Indians continued to attack, however, at several points throughout the day and eventually surrounded the whole British force. Bouquet then opened up his files and moved some of the troops to make it appear as if they were retreating. The Indians, sensing an advantage, proceeded to attack at which point the British troops closed in from the flanks. The remaining troops turned and met the Indians head-on, causing them to flee. The British lost fifty men, while about sixty Indians, including several chiefs, were killed. The British returned to their encampment at Bushy Run, where the Indians attacked and were again dispersed. With the defeat of the Indians at the Battle of Bushy Run (Figures 114 and 115), the British continued to Fort Pitt unimpeded and replenished that post.

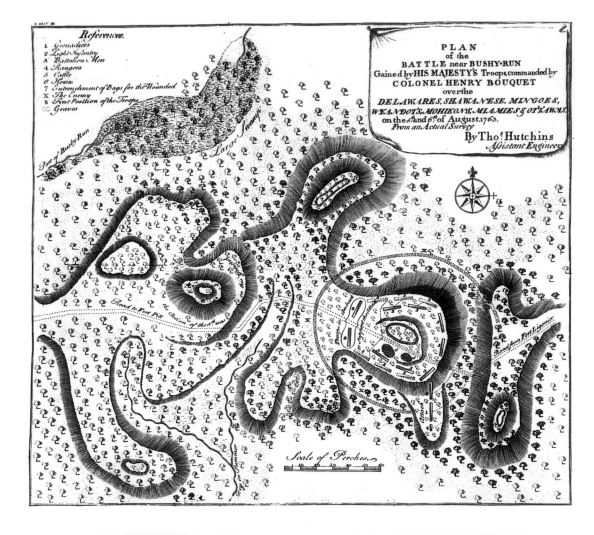

Figure 115.

The Battle of Bushy Run. Four plans: (1) Encampment; (2) Disposition to receive the Enemy; (3) Line of March; (4) General Attack. In [William Smith] *A Historical Account of the Expedition against the Ohio Indians in the Year MDCCLXIV.* London: Thomas Jefferys, 1766. (Personal Collection.)

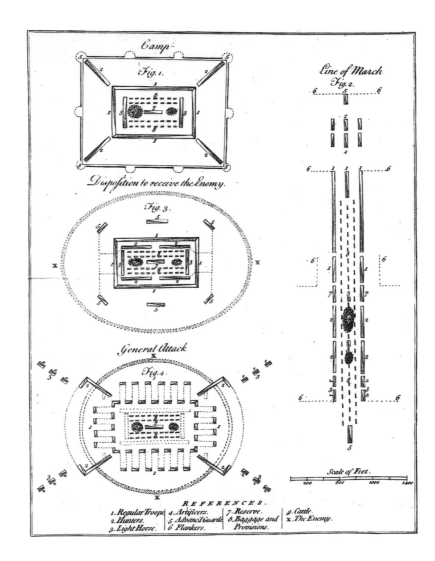

On September 3rd a schooner carrying provisions from Niagara entered the Detroit River. That evening it was attacked by 350 Indians in canoes. A fierce fight ensued, but the Indians were repelled and food was thus provided to the famished garrison. The Indians dedicated to obstructing communications between Fort Niagara and Lake Erie were simultaneously routed by troops from Niagara. Thus the three major forts—Pitt, Detroit, and Niagara—had their positions strengthened and the effectiveness of the Indians' activities was reduced.

On April 3, 1764, at Johnson Hall in the Mohawk Valley of New York, Sir William Johnson, who held the position of Superintendent of Indian Affairs for northern North America, signed a peace treaty with the Seneca nation. General Thomas Gage, who had succeeded General Jeffrey Amherst as commander in chief, sent Colonel John Bradstreet and a show of force of over one thousand men to the south shore of Lake Erie to complete the submission of the Indians in that region. On August 12th the Delawares, Hurons, and the Five Nations of the Scioto Plains sued for peace. On September 7th at Detroit Bradstreet formalized a peace treaty with the Ottawas and Chippewas.

The third element in the petitions for peace with the Indians was executed by Colonel Bouquet, who left Fort Pitt on October 3rd with fifteen hundred men. They marched to the Muskingum River (Figure 116) conducting a series of peace conferences with Indian tribes (Figure 117), which returned many hostages taken in the past (Figure 118). The mission was completed on November 18th and the troops returned to Fort Pitt ten days later, at which time Indian prisoners in the fort were released as a gesture of peace. This brought down the curtain on the Indian component of the French and Indian War and left the North American continent free from battles for a decade. At that time yet another curtain arose—the War of the American Revolution, or the War of Independence.

Figure 116.

The West.
"A General Map of the Country on the Ohio and Muskingham Shewing the Situations of the Indian=Towns with respect to the Army under the Command of Colonel Bouquet... A Topographical Plan of that part of the Indian=Country through which the Army under the Command of Colonel Bouquet marched in the Year 1764. Thos. Hutchins, Asst. Engineer." Engraved, 57 x 50 cm. The top map shows Forts Loudoun, Lyttelton, Cumberland, and Bedford, General Braddock's Field, Colonel Bouquet's Field, Fort Pitt, Fort Le Boeuf, Fort Presque Isle, and Fort Sandusky. The second map shows the sixteen encampments from Fort Pitt to the Forks of the Muskingum. In *An Historical Account of the Expedition against the Ohio Indians, in the Year 1764...* [By William Smith]. Philadelphia: William Bradford, 1765. (Personal Collection.)

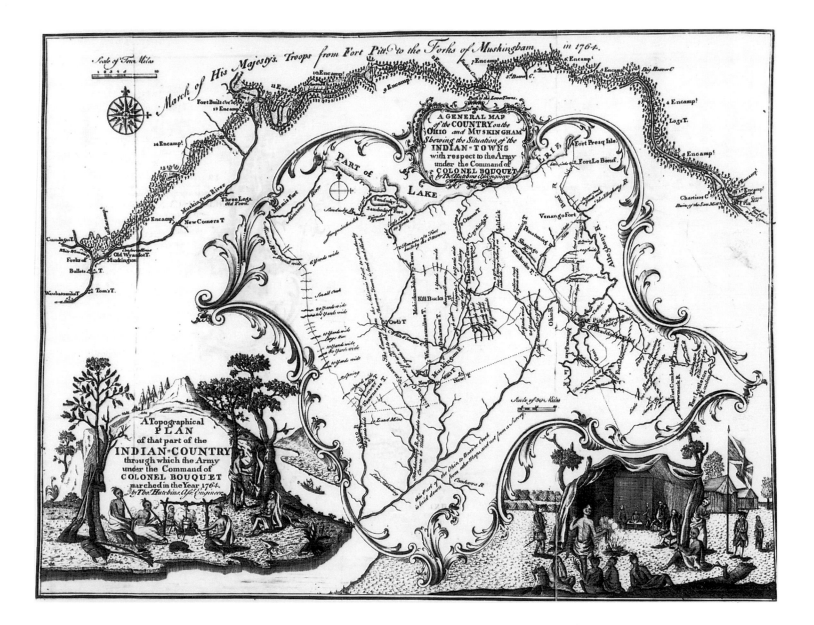

March of His Majesty's Troops from Fort Pitt, to the Forks of Muskingham in 1764.

A GENERAL MAP of the COUNTRY on the OHIO and MUSKINGHAM Shewing the Situation of the INDIAN-TOWNS with respect to the Army under the Command of COLONEL BOUQUET by Thos Hutchins Assistant Engineer

A Topographical PLAN of that part of the INDIAN-COUNTRY through which the Army under the Command of COLONEL BOUQUET marched in the Year 1764. By Thos Hutchins Ass Engineer

Figure 117.

Peace talks.
"The Indians giving a Talk to Colonel Bouquet in a Conference at a Council Fire near his Camp on the Banks of the Muskingum in North America in Octr. 1764." Engraving after painting by Benjamin West. Engraved by Grignion, 20 x 16 cm. In [William Smith] *An Historical Account of the Expedition against the Ohio Indians in the Year MDCCLXIV.* London: Thomas Jefferys, 1766. (Personal Collection.)

Figure 118.

Release of captives. "The Indians delivering up the English Captives to Colonel Bouquet near his camp at the Forks of Muskingum in North American in November 1764." Engraving by Canot after Benjamin West. In [William Smith] *An Historical Account of the Expedition against the Ohio Indians in the Year* MDCCLXIV. London: Thomas Jefferys, 1766. (Personal Collection.)

Bibliography

Eighteenth-Century Publications

An Accurate and Authentic Journal of the Siege of Quebec, 1759. By a Gentleman in an eminent Station on the Spot. London: J. Robinson, 1759.

An Authentic Account of the Reduction of Louisbourg, in June and July 1758. By a Spectator. London: W. Owen, 1758.

[Huske, John.] *The Present State of North America, &c.* Part I. 2d ed., with emendations. London: R. and J. Dodsley, 1755.

Knox, Captain John. *An Historical Journal of the Campaigns in North America, For the Years 1757, 1758, 1759, and 1760.* London: n.p., 1769.

Mante, Thomas. *The History of the Late War in North-America, and the Islands of the West-Indies, including the Campaigns of 1763 and 1764 with His Majesty's Indian Enemies.* London: W. Strahan and T. Cadell, 1772.

Pouchot, Pierre. *Mémoires sur La Derniere Guerre de l'Amérique Septentrionale entre la France et l'Angleterre.* Yverdon, Switzerland, 1781.

[Rocque, John.] *A Set of Plans and Forts in America. Reduced from Actual Surveys.* London: Mary Rocque, 1763.

Rogers, Robert. *Journals of Major Robert Rogers.* London: n.p., 1765.

[Smith, William.] *An Historical Account of the Expedition against the Ohio Indians, in the Year 1764.* Under the Command of Henry Bouquet, Esq:. Philadelphia: William Bradford, 1765.

[Washington, George.] *The Journal of Major George Washington.* Williamsburg, Virginia, 1754.

Nineteenth- and Twentieth-Century Publications

Alberts, Robert C. *The Most Extraordinary Adventures of Major Robert Stobo*. Boston: Houghton Mifflin, 1965.

Berkeley, Edmund, and Dorothy Smith Berkeley. Dr. John Mitchell: *The Man Who Made the Map of North America*. Chapel Hill: University of North Carolina Press, 1974.

[Bougainville, Louis-Antoine de.] *Adventures in the Wilderness: The American Journals of Louis-Antoine de Bougainville, 1756–1760*. Edward P. Hamilton, ed. Norman: University of Oklahoma, 1964.

Brown, Lloyd. *Early Maps of the Ohio Valley*. Pittsburgh: University of Pittsburgh, 1959.

Cleland, Hugh. *George Washington in the Ohio Valley*. Pittsburgh: University of Pittsburgh, 1955.

Cuneo, John R. *Robert Rogers of the Rangers*. New York: Oxford Unversity Press, 1959.

Darlington, William M., ed. *Christopher Gist's Journals with Historical, Geographical, and Ethnological Notes and Biographies of His Contemporaries*. Pittsburgh: n.p., 1893.

Eckert, Allen W. *Wilderness Empire: A Narrative*. Boston: Little, Brown, 1969.

Ferling, John E. *A Wilderness of Miseries: War and Warriors in Early America*. Westport, Connecticut, 1980.

Flexner, James Thomas. *Mohawk Baronet: Sir William Johnson of New York*. Boston: Little, Brown, 1959.

Freeman, Douglas Southall. *George Washington: A Biography*. Vols. 1 and 2. New York: Scribners, 1951.

Gipson, Lawrence Henry. *The British Empire Before the American Revolution*. Vols. 5–8. New York: Knopf, 1930–1961.

Hamilton, Charles, ed. Braddock's Defeat: *The Journals of Captain Robert Chomley's Batman; The Journal of a British Officer; Halkett's Orderly Book.* Norman, Oklahoma, 1959.

Harrington, J. C. *New Light on Washington's Fort Necessity.* Richmond: Eastern National Park and Monument Association, 1957.

Jackson, Donald, ed. *The Diaries of George Washington, 1748–1799.* 6 vols. Charlottesville, Virginia, 1976 79.

Jennings, Francis. *Empire of Fortune.* New York: Norton, 1988.

Keegley, F. B. *Keegley's Virginia Frontier: The Beginning of the Southwest, the Roanoke of Colonial Days, 1740–1783*, with Maps and Illustrations. Roanoke, Virginia, 1938.

Lawrence, Parker King. "Anglo-American Wilderness Campaigning, 1754–1764: Logistical and Tactical Developments." Ph.D. diss., Columbia University, 1970.

Leach, Douglas Edward. *Arms for Empire: A Military History of the British Colonies in North America, 1607–1763.* New York: Macmillan, 1973.

Lloyd, Christopher. *The Capture of Quebec.* New York: Macmillan, 1959.

Long, J. C. *Lord Jeffrey Amherst, A Soldier of the King.* New York: Macmillan, 1933.

Pargellis, Stanley M. "Braddock's Defeat." In *American Historical Review*, Vol. 41, No. 2 (Jan. 1936): 253–269.

Pargellis, Stanley M., *Military Affairs in North America, 1748–1765: Selected Documents from the Cumberland Papers in Windsor Castle.* New York, 1936; reprint, New York, 1969.

Parkman, Francis. *Montcalm and Wolfe.* Boston: Little, Brown, 1909.

Sargent, Winthrop, ed. *The History of an Expedition against Fort Duquesne in 1755 under Major-General Edward Braddock.* Philadelphia, Pennsylvania, 1855.

Titus, James. *The Old Dominion at War: Society, Politics & Warfare in Late Colonial Virginia*. Columbia, S.C.: University of South Carolina Press, 1991.

The George Washington Atlas. Lawrence Martin, ed. Washington, D.C.: U.S. George Washington Bicentennial Commission, 1932.

Index

Index

Page numbers in *italics* refer to maps, illustrations, and related legends.